W9-BZI-530

^TE DUE

Twayne's United States Authors Series

EDITOR OF THIS VOLUME

Kenneth Eble

University of Utah

Ezra Pound

TUSAS 348

EZRA POUND

By James F. Knapp

University of Pittsburgh

TWAYNE PUBLISHERS

A DIVISION OF G.K. HALL & CO., BOSTON

Copyright © 1979 by G. K. Hall & Co.

Published in 1979 by Twayne Publishers,
A Division of G. K. Hall & Co.
All Rights Reserved

Printed on permanent/durable acid-free paper and bound
in the United States of America

Frontispiece photo of Ezra Pound reproduced with permission of
Humanities Research Center, The University of Texas at Austin.

Austin Community College
Learning Resources Center

Library of Congress Cataloging in Publication Data

Knapp, James F
Ezra Pound.

(Twayne's United States authors series ; TUSAS 348)
Bibliography: p. 168–73
Includes index.
1. Pound, Ezra Loomis,1885–1972—Criticism and interpretation.
PS3531.082Z714   811'.5'2   79–14762
ISBN 0-8057-7286-3

For Peggy

Contents

About the Author

James F. Knapp received his Ph.D. from the University of Connecticut in 1966, writing a dissertation on contemporary British poetry. In that year he joined the English Department at the University of Pittsburgh, where he is currently an associate professor, and director of the literature program.

Professor Knapp has published a number of articles on modern and contemporary poetry, but his scholarly and teaching interests are wide ranging. He has also written on medieval romance, myth theory, popular culture, pedagogy, and, most recently, on the possible impact of the humanities on the study of the future. Among the journals in which his articles have appeared are *Modern Language Quarterly, The Sewanee Review, Twentieth Century Literature, The Centennial Review,* and *College English.*

Preface

Few poets in the twentieth century have been as difficult to read, or to write about, as Ezra Pound. As a man, Pound was nearly always involved in controversy, and by World War II that controversy had become very bitter. Many of the books about Pound have focused on his life, sometimes to condemn his failings, but more often to justify his character and his vision in the face of charges that he had betrayed his country. The issue is important, and Pound's life may be seen as emblematic of much of the aspiration, and the tragedy, of our century. But a great deal has already been written about Pound the man, and in such studies the poetry, quite naturally, receives little attention. Although I have not ignored the events of Pound's life, my own aim has been, rather, to trace the developing patterns of his thought and art. The story of that process is my subject, and when I draw on biography I do so in hopes of clarifying the poems and the essays in light of their ultimate origin in Pound's long struggle to know his world.

In setting out to avoid the temptation to spend too much time on the complexities of Pound's life, I have also attempted to avoid the other extreme which the complexity of his work invites. Much of the criticism which has focused on the works themselves has tended to become very specialized, even arcane, exploring all the implications of particular references and motifs in the poetry, without offering a full sense of the larger patterns of meaning. However necessary to a full exegesis of Pound's work, such books are written primarily for a very restricted audience of other specialists. My own aim has been to avoid that extreme as well, and to suggest instead that when the poetry is seen whole, all of it, it reveals a coherent intellectual quest, of central importance to our time. Quite simply, my thesis is that Pound began his career in a nineteenth-century world which came apart before his eyes, and that when he set out to build it new he began a process decades long. Distressed by the artistic sterility of his age, and then increasingly by the economic oppression which he saw all around him, Pound searched for a better way. Through decades of sifting past and present in search of moments worth recreating, he came finally to a vision of the earth which sustains us all, a vision of natural order lost for too many centuries in the egocentric greed and exploitation of history.

The pursuit of that vision began early and continued steadily through many years. I would argue that there is a coherence in Pound's work which links his earliest lyric and his last, fragmentary canto. Accordingly, my approach to the poetry is chronological, tracing the successive exploration of new poetic techniques which was Pound's way of learning to see the world fresh. To understand the characteristic thought, as well as the gradually changing form, of the shorter poems collected in *Personae* is by far the most natural way of access to *The Cantos,* and I have treated them at some length. In *The Cantos,* however, Pound began to work in a form which yields little to a simple chronological reading. The meaning of that long poem begins to appear only gradually, as Pound introduces motifs and then, over a space of many cantos, repeats and transforms them, slowly combining isolated events and images into more inclusive patterns. Though my discussion of *The Cantos* does move, generally, from early cantos to late, my chief aim is to make clear the poem's technique, and its major concerns. To that end I have often drawn together images from widely separated cantos so that the crucial patterns which exist only through these clusters of detail can be more easily seen. If such an approach can by no means be a full explication of this enormous, rich poem, it does serve to introduce the reader to Pound's unique way of organizing his perceptions. And when the poem is regarded in this way, without demanding of it a more traditional plot or logic, then the shape of Pound's search for new ways to know an altered world becomes unmistakable.

JAMES F. KNAPP

University of Pittsburgh

Acknowledgments

By permission of New Directions Publishing Corporation, I quote
from the following works of Ezra Pound:

Personae. Copyright 1926 by Ezra Pound.

The Cantos. Copyright 1934, 1937, 1940, 1948, © 1956, © 1959,
© 1966 by Ezra Pound.

The Selected Letters of Ezra Pound (1907-1941), edited by D. D.
Paige. Copyright 1950 by Ezra Pound.

Literary Essays. Copyright 1918, 1920, 1935 by Ezra Pound.

The Spirit of Romance. All Rights Reserved. Copyright © 1968
by Ezra Pound.

Selected Prose, 1909-1965, edited by William Cookson.
Copyright © 1973 by the Estate of Ezra Pound. All Rights
Reserved.

By permission of St. Martin's Press, Inc., Macmillan & Co., Ltd.,
I quote from *The Battle of Maldon and Other Old English Poems,*
translated by Kevin Crossley-Holland and edited by Bruce
Mitchell; copyright Kevin Crossley-Holland and Bruce Mitchell.

Frontispiece courtesy Humanities Research Center, The
University of Texas at Austin.

Chronology

	Land. The Natural Philosophy of Love, by Remy de Gourmont, translated and introduced by Pound.
1923	*Indiscretions, or Une revue de deux mondes.*
1924	Moves to Rapallo, in Italy. *Anthiel and the Treatise on Harmony.*
1925	*A Draft of XVI Cantos.* July 9, daughter, Mary, born to Pound and Olga Rudge.
1926	*Personae: The Collected Poems of Ezra Pound.* September 10, son, Omar Shakespear Pound born.
1928	*A Draft of the Cantos 17-27. Ta Hio, The Great Learning. Selected Poems*, with introduction by T. S. Eliot.
1930	*A Draft of XXX Cantos. Imaginary Letters.*
1931	*How to Read.*
1932	*Guido Cavalcanti Rime.*
1933	Edits *Active Anthology. ABC of Economics.*
1934	*Eleven New Cantos, XXXI-XLI. ABC of Reading. Make It New.*
1935	*Alfred Venison's Poems. Jefferson and/or Mussolini. Social Credit: An Impact.*
1937	*The Fifth Decad of The Cantos. Polite Essays.*
1938	*Guide to Kulchur.*
1939	Visit to U.S., honorary D.Litt. from Hamilton College.
1940	*Cantos LII-LXXI.*
1941	Began regular broadcasts over Rome Radio.
1943	Indicted for treason by the United States.
1945	Arrested by U.S. Army, and held as prisoner for six months at the Disciplinary Training Center at Pisa. November, flown to Washington, D.C.
1946	Declared unfit to stand trial on account of insanity, committed to St. Elizabeth's Hospital, Washington, D.C.
1947	*Confucius: The Unwobbling Pivot and The Great Digest.*
1948	*The Pisan Cantos. The Cantos. If This Be Treason.*
1949	Bollingen Prize for *The Pisan Cantos.*
1953	*The Translations of Ezra Pound.*
1954	*The Classical Anthology Defined by Confucius.*
1955	*Section: Rock Drill, 85-95 de los cantares.* (Milan)
1956	*Sophokles: Women of Trachis.*
1958	Indictment for treason dismissed, released from St. Elizabeth's, returns to Italy.
1959	*Thrones: 96-109 de los cantares.*

Chronology

CHAPTER 1

Poetry and Vision

I Starting Out in America

EZRA Pound was born an American, and through all the long years of a life lived in exile, he remained one. He was born in 1885, in Hailey, Idaho, a gold town in the raw West, and he used that credential to prove to his friend William Carlos Williams that no amount of international culture and Mediterranean sun could ever damage his intuitive grasp of the American experience. His father had been in charge of the United States Land Office in Hailey, while his grandfather, Thaddeus, was a successful lumberman and one-time lieutenant governor of Wisconsin. Among his ancestors were Pennsylvania Quakers, and New York State horse thieves, and the poet Henry Wadsworth Longfellow. In 1889, the family moved to Philadelphia where Homer Pound became assistant assayer at the United States Mint. They lived in the city at first, but by the time Ezra was six, they had bought a large house in nearby Wyncote, complete with a vegetable garden and a swing in the apple tree. Pound lived there for the next sixteen years, growing up into a world of comfortable gentility and modest culture. It was among those wide-porched white houses that his early memories of life in America were formed, and it was there that he heard stories about Thaddeus Pound issuing his own Union Lumbering Company money. He visited the Mint with his father, played in the hills around Wyncote, and began to learn about the world beyond Philadelphia.

By the time he was fifteen, Pound had decided to be a poet, and in the fall of that year he enrolled at the University of Pennsylvania, where he studied for two years before transferring to Hamilton College, in upstate New York, in 1903. He completed his undergraduate study at Hamilton, and returned to the University of Pennsylvania in 1905 to begin work for his master's degree in Romance languages. Already, most of the major concerns of his later intellectual life had been discovered, with the help of a few professors whom he continued to mention forty years later, in letters and in *The Cantos:* Felix E. Schelling, Cornelius Weygandt, Hugo A. Rennert at Pennsylvania; William Pierce Shepard and Joseph Darling Ibbotson at Hamilton. He continued his study of Latin and began to learn German, French, Spanish, and Italian; alongside classical literature, the Middle Ages became a focus for his reading, particularly Anglo-Saxon, Middle English, Provençal, and Tuscan poetry; and in Dr. Weygandt's seminar, he began to read the verse of his immediate predecessors in the English nineties. Another undergraduate subject, which was to remain dormant in Pound's mind for some years, before it too became a vital passion, was the study of American political history. Among the friends he made during those years were William Carlos Williams, the painter William Brooke Smith, and Hilda Doolittle ("H.D."), to whom he was briefly, and rather informally, engaged. With Williams, he immediately began a friendship which involved lifelong argument about the principles of art. Against Pound's growing cosmopolitanism, Williams set his own need to probe the local details of his experience of America, and their dialogue, strained and crotchety at times, occupied five decades of reviews, articles, and letters. And for Hilda Doolittle, Pound made his first book of verse in 1907. He called it *Hilda's Book*, and he made it literally, sewing it in vellum with his own hands. Of the poems in that book, only one is of interest now, but it still opens the volume of his collected shorter poems,[1] and it says much about where Ezra Pound began: "I stood still and was a tree amid the wood, / Knowing the truth of things unseen before." "The Tree," with its occasionally archaic diction ("Nathless"), and heavily romantic alliteration and internal rhyme ("Unto the hearth of their heart's home"), seems far from what we have come to know as modern poetry, and yet the language is mostly rather simple and direct. With its reference to Daphne and its use of classical myth as occasion for reverie, the poem seems a thing of the nineteenth century. But little else could be expected of one of Pound's earliest poems, and more significant for understanding the work to come is what, in an old tradition, has interested him. More than anything else, this is a poem about the importance of point of view. A kind of slight exercise in Ovid's *Metamorphoses*, modified by Robert Browning's dramatic monologue, "The Tree" emphasizes the subjective experience, rather than the physical action, of a radical change of form. Cézanne had already painted a picture whose perspective seemed to suggest that we were viewing a table both from above and below, at the same time; while in literature, Henry James was demonstrating how the world we know alters with altering points of view. Later, Joyce, Faulkner, Beckett, and many other modernist writers would carry those insights much further, shaping their works around the principle that the world we know is, at least in part, a function of our own limited perspectives. Ezra Pound in 1907, however, was not interested in the philosophical implications of this notion, nor in the social implications of a world of men and women isolated in the prisons of their own subjectivity, and so failing to communicate in any human way with each other — the topic of absurdist drama later in the century. His interest was in the experience itself, the overwhelming feeling of becoming something other, and learning to know the world in that new way. For the speaker, who has been transformed into a tree, the poem's topic is "knowing," but for Pound, it is the powerful *emotion* of wonder and discovery which accompanies the knowing that is the poem's true subject.

Catching the mood and emotion of an event in some dim mythic past, "The Tree" is typical of the poetic concerns which Pound encountered during his student years. In 1915 he wrote an introduction to the works of Lionel Johnson in which he recalled the literary enthusiasms of that time: "In America ten or twelve years ago one read Fiona MacLeod, and Dowson, and Symons. One was guided by Mr. Mosher of Bangor. I think I first heard of Johnson in an odd sort of post-graduate course conducted by Dr. Weygandt. One was drunk with 'Celticism,' and with Dowson's 'Cynara,' and with one or two poems of Symons' 'Wanderers' and 'I am the torch she saith.' "[2] That poetry of the nineties had been highly "aesthetic," rejecting the materialism (and lack of taste) of the Victorian era, and turning instead to the contemplation of Beauty—sought in subtle moods and momentary glimpses. The setting might well be a city, London or Paris perhaps, but there was no sociological ugliness, no sordid detail, only the moment of strangely distanced beauty, set down in precise, languid, evocative verse. It was symbolist poetry, transferred to English soil, but preserving Verlaine's injunction, in his "Art Poétique," to write verse that is at once vague and precise. Language must be used with meticulous care, so as to suggest, not the lines of the physical world, but the ideal beyond matter. George Moore expressed the symbolist attitude toward the world of appearance, and writers who concerned themselves with that world, as well as anyone: "The thing itself is worthless; and the moral writers who embellish it with pious ornamentation are just as reprehensible as Zola, who embellishes it with erotic arabesques. You want the idea drawn out of obscuring matter, this can best be done by the symbol."[3].

This artistic stance led to a poetry of evocation, of harmonious sound and image intended to lead the reader to a perception of beauty no longer present to the bourgeois consciousness. And, in poem's like Pound's "In Durance," it led to a presentation of the artist as an isolated being, in touch with a nonmaterial beauty which speaks through spirits to his soul, but alienated from the mass of men and women who cannot see such visions. The poem assumes a tone of wistful sadness mixed with disdain ("ordinary people touch me not"), and the rejection of all but those initiated into the mysteries of art is accompanied by an appropriate vagueness surrounding the spirits, who are called, in suggestive italics, *"they."* In presenting his speaker as "flesh-shrouded, bearing the secret," Pound not only expresses an almost Manichean loathing of physical body, but he affirms the sacred nature of art as preserver of divine secrets. The sense of flesh as an obstacle to be purged away so that the ideal might be seen more clearly was a pose for Pound in 1907, and within a short time he would begin to denounce that notion as one of the first perversions of Western culture. But the desire to see beyond the surface of things to some ineffable world of forms was more lasting, and continued through the latest *Cantos.* "In Durance" ends on that note of uncompleted yearning ("Beyond, beyond, beyond, there lies . . .") and that aspect of the symbolist aesthetic would stay with Pound long after the fashion for symbolist verse had passed.

A more personal aspect of "In Durance" involves the particular time in Pound's life when it was written. In the fall of 1907, he left his doctoral studies at the University of Pennsylvania to take a position as instructor of Romance languages at Wabash College in Crawfordsville, Indiana. From the outset, his experience was an unhappy one, as the pose of isolated artist, which he had learned in the symbolist poetry he read, was reinforced every day by the suspicions of a small midwestern town unimpressed by his bohemian airs. By the middle of the school year, Pound had managed to create a minor scandal by letting a stranded showgirl spend the night in his rooms. Accounts of the event differ, but the result was that by February, Pound was sailing for Europe, the college having been delighted to buy his contract in exchange for a quick departure. In Indiana, he had encountered what seemed to him a terribly narrow provincialism, and the European culture which had been the object of his studies suddenly became a clear alternative in his eyes, a possible new way of life.

II *London*

Pound had already visited Europe three times, his most recent trip being in 1906 when he went to the libraries and museums of London, Paris, and Madrid as a student of medieval literature. He had seen Venice on previous trips, and it was to that city, whose decrepit splendor had already begun to seem symbolic of a lost culture worth seeking again, that he came in 1908. He had his first volume of poetry, *A Lume Spento,* privately printed there, and he stayed on for three months, trying to find some way to make a living. But his real destination, if he was serious about breaking into the literary world, was London, and by September he knew it, and left Venice. Pound came to London with a conception of poetry shaped by the poets of the nineties whom he had read in Philadelphia, and by a few older figures— Browning, Rossetti, Swinburne. In a poem such as "De Aegypto," from *A Lume Spento,* for instance, he had made use of Rossetti's syntax and alluded to one of his stories.[4] The poem is typical of Pound's early interests: the painter of Rossetti's story, who had watched his soul appear to him as a woman, becomes a writer, and he in turn is combined with Aegyptus, inheritor of Arabia and conqueror of Egypt, to make a kind of conqueror of spirit kingdoms. There is no plot beyond this simple evocation of the artist's power to attain a perception of "the Lady of Life," unhindered by the body's bounds. With its soft, evocative diction, its symbols capitalized, and its presentation of the artist as priest of the mysteries, "De Aegypto" carries on the romanticism of the later nineteenth century.

In the poems which Pound wrote for a number of years after arriving in London, that romanticism continued to appear. Sometimes the result was a very slight poem about momentary experience — in "Erat Hora" (*P*, 40), for example, the speaker has glimpsed that mysterious lady who serves so often in Pound's early work to suggest a transient spiritual beauty. She vanishes amid images of leaves turning away from sun, in wind, and the speaker simply gives thanks for having seen his brief vision. The poem's basic device — a moment of rare, meaningful personal experience, set down briefly and simply — is a familiar convention of the nineteenth century, but for Pound it became more than just a form to be imitated while learning his craft. In the imagist theories which he was soon to formulate, and in the far more innovative achievement of his *Cantos*, this emphasis on isolated moments of perception, charged with meaning as well as emotion, became not only a way to knowing, but a basic principle of artistic structure.

Of those poets of the English decadent movement who had given Pound his first models, none was more present to his imagination on arriving in London than William Butler Yeats, who had survived the nineties to flourish in the new century as few of that group had. Pound hoped to meet Yeats, and eventually he did, the two poets finding a friendship of mutual advice and criticism which lasted until Yeats' death in 1939. The influence of Yeats' verse is often present in Pound's early work, but perhaps the clearest example is "The White Stag" (*P*, 25):

> I ha' seen them 'mid the clouds on the heather.
> Lo! they pause not for love nor for sorrow,
> Yet their eyes are as the eyes of a maid to her lover,
> When the white hart breaks his cover
> And the white wind breaks the morn.

The brief visionary experience which Pound had drawn from a dozen sources in nineteenth-century romanticism takes place here in a setting borrowed from the Celtic strain of Arthurian romance. The mysterious Lady becomes Malory's white stag (though still with "the eyes of a maid"), a fairy messenger from some immortal realm who only appears to the few chosen mortals. But despite the heather and the suggestion of Celtic myth, the basic situation once again involves a mortal man yearning to attain some ineffable quality, expressed in evocative symbol, which he has seen during a brief transcendence of his human limitations. And the language is pure Yeats, in effects like that created, at the end of the passage I have quoted, by the repetition "white heart breaks" / "white wind breaks" in two successive lines, the rhythm carrying quickly over the unstressed syllables which end the first line and begin the second, only to enter an apparent repeat which is brought up short by the change to a clearly final stress on "morn." When Pound later wrote of being "drunk with Celticism" during his university days, he shed some light on the origin of poems like this one.

Celticism was not really what Yeats could offer Pound, however. The younger poet was seeking a style, and he'was also seeking a symbolic language capable of expressing the values which were beginning to cohere for him. "The White Stag" tested the possibilities of a large body of traditional symbol, resurrected in large part through the efforts of Yeats, Lady Gregory, and the other members of the Irish Renaissance. But Pound was also looking elsewhere for his symbolic language, and he found a more promising image in the city which first drew him back to Europe, after Crawfordsville. Venice is the subject of "Night Litany" (*P*, 26), a poem whose occasion is simply the contemplation of that city's image reflected in her waters at night. The poet regards, not the city itself, but the city's reflection in the water, and that reflected image of beauty is really only the shadow of a shadow. In a Platonic sense of successive removals from true reality, Pound assumes God as primary, so that the beauty of Venice becomes a shadow of the Divine, visible to mortal eyes, and even the most tenuous reflection of that shadow, in dark waters, is capable of evoking an awesome sense of its ultimate source. The poem's theme is still based on the symbolist desire to find images which evoke a beauty beyond matter, but in its specific choice of an object, "Night Litany" locates a symbol whose implications Pound could explore for years to come. The city can be at once an object of great physical beauty, a way of learning to perceive Divine presence in the mortal world, and—most important for his later poetry—a complex matrix of human civilization, a visible sign of the possibility of a society which fuses simple earthly justice with the vision of Divine beauty.

Even in poems like "Praise of Ysolt" (*P*, 16), where the Celtic subject matter of Yeats is prominent, Pound was combining precedents and experimenting with his own poetic voice. "Praise of Ysolt" takes little more than the name of its heroine from the Tristan legend, but it does draw deeply on the traditions of Celtic nature poetry and magic. The mysterious Lady who represents beauty, and who calls the poet to his art, is made to be "a woman of the wonder-folk," a Celtic fairy. And the poem is filled with images of nature, a nature which speaks to the poet, offering him words which may constitute the link between his isolated humanity and the larger living world of which he is a part:

> The words are as leaves, old brown leaves in the spring time
> Blowing they know not whither, seeking a song.
>
> White words as snow flakes but they are cold,
> Moss words, lip words, words of slow streams.

If the tradition of the word as standing between man and nature, in the poet's power to communicate vital relationship, is ancient and Celtic (and perhaps Orphic as well), it also became a principle which was increasingly important to Pound, especially after he had begun to write *The Cantos*. In his later thought, the entire world seemed to be infused with an intelligence which might be read, and brought to focused perception in language, but that belief was already present in this experiment in Celticism, from the very first volume of poetry he published.

In addition to its Celtic manner, though, "Praise of Ysolt" also draws on another of Pound's early interests. Basically still a simple, lyrical utterance, there is nevertheless some suggestion of a more particular characterization, and the "plot" and setting are more fully developed than in those briefer poems which simply record the perception of a moment. Pound's Tristan-poet, separated from the Ysolt who is his muse, takes on the character of a rather dejected, travel-worn vagabond. And while "Praise of Ysolt" is no real exploration of character, it does stand as a kind of link between Pound's poems concerned with the perception of a transcendent beauty, derived chiefly from Yeats and the decadents, and beyond them, Rossetti, and those poems deriving from the other important nineteenth-century influence on Pound's verse: the dramatic monologue of Robert Browning.

III   *From Tennyson to Browning*

When Pound arrived in London in 1908, he came with the expectation of finding the literary world he had slowly been putting together in his head—Yeats and the nineties, Rossetti, Swinburne, Browning, perhaps some interest in medieval song and classical verse. But the scene he found was very different indeed, and profoundly disheartening. The nineties were dead, Yeats more or less an isolated voice, and the poetry reading public firmly in the hands of a kind of rhetorical John Bull versifier:

> You in high places; you that drive the steeds
> Of Empire; you that say unto your hosts,
> "Go thither," and they go; and from our coasts
> Bid sail the squadrons, and they sail, their deeds
> Shaking the world. . . .[5]

This passage from William Watson is typical of the sort of verse made enormously popular by poets like Maurice Hewlett, Henry Newbolt, Rudyard Kipling, and Alfred Noyes. For Pound, their work represented everything that was bad about the Victorian heritage, with its patriotic defense of progress, empire, and public values. The inflated rhetoric of passages like this one seemed to mask the emptiness of received opinions which were little better than official propaganda, and which ignored, or rejected outright, everything he held dear: the examination of private experience, the quest for Beauty, the cultivation of a language sufficiently precise and evocative to release that visionary perception of a reality lying beyond the tawdry matter of Victoria's workshop.

For Pound, the evils of nineteenth-century verse were most easily illustrated by the work of Alfred Lord Tennyson, who could write lines like these:

> And here the singer for his art
> Not all in vain may plead
> "The song that nerves a nation's heart
> Is in itself a deed."

This "Epilogue to the Charge of the Heavy Brigade" represents a kind of poetry whose chief technical concern is to achieve a stirring rhetoric, and whose conception of the social usefulness of poetry is that it should inspire the reader to help achieve nationally defined goals. Art is subservient to society, acting as a medium of expression for public rather than private interests, and adopting a style appropriate to that function: discursive, generalizing, rhetorically moving, and never obscure or overly demanding. Pound spoke of "the Victorian cult of the innocuous" when he discussed the course of nineteenth-century poetry, and Tennyson was a central example:

"Is it credible that his (Tennyson's) whole mind should be made up of fine sentiments," says Bagehot. Of course it wasn't. It was that lady-like attitude toward the printed page that did it—that something, that ineffable "something," which kept Tennyson out of his works. When he began to write for Viccy's ignorant ear, he immediately ceased to be the "Tennyson so muzzy that he tried to go out through the fireplace," the Tennyson with the broad North accent, the old man with the worst manners in England (except Carlyle's), the Tennyson whom "it kept the whole combined efforts of his family and his publishers to keep respectable." He became the Tate Gallery among poets.[6]

As Pound saw it, Tennyson was by no means a man without talent, but rather a poet corrupted by the demands of the respectable, public world for which he increasingly came to write. What Pound could have admired—the cranky particularity of the man—was not allowed into the poems, which were made for stately display, like the room after room of heroic battles and formal landscapes at the Tate Gallery, where the history of English painting is hung.

But if Pound's rejection of the nineteenth century was a violent one, it was never simple. He did admire the genius of Wordsworth "for imagisme, for a presentation of natural detail", while at the same time denouncing him as "a silly old sheep."[7] And his assessment of Tennyson was essentially the same: a lyrical gift, and the potential for making good poems out of the rich detail of his own character, spoiled by a public taste which called for moralizing rhetoric. It was the notion of poetry as versified moral essay that Pound rejected, and when he found a poet willing to leave the language of public speech to explore the unique detail of individual lives, in words tuned to their function,

he was ready enough to praise, and imitate. Robert Browning
was such a poet, and Pound valued his example. In 1917 he wrote
that "the most interesting poems in Victorian English are
Browning's *Men and Women,* or, if that statement is too absolute,
let me contend that the form of these poems is the most vital
form of that period of English, and that the poems written in that
form are the least like each other in content."[8] Although he
qualified his praise in that essay by noting that Browning
"included a certain amount of ratiocination and of purely
intellectual comment, and in just that proportion he lost
intensity," the influence of Browning's dramatic monologues on
Pound's early poetry was considerable. When Browning was not
indulging in that "ratiocination" which seemed to Pound to be
the downfall of Victorian poetry, he offered the example of an
exploration of individual experience which valued the particular
and the concrete, and which was a natural corollary to Pound's
interest in the precise nuances of subjective experience. In
Pound's earliest volume of poetry, those delicate symbolist
exercises in capturing the emotion of moments exist side by side
with poems like "Cino," "Famam Librosque Cano," and "La
Fraisne," which test the possibilities of a poetry based on the
communication of unfamiliar experience by means of specific
details, precisely rendered, but without comment.

"Paracelsus in Excelsis" is a poem which responds directly to
Browning's "Paracelsus," though in its form it is closer to the
brief lyric reveries which Pound was writing at the same time
than it is to the more fully developed dramatic monologue. The
poem is interesting, however, because it offers the thoughts of a
sixteenth-century alchemist whose successful escape from the
world of matter is identical with the symbolist quest to penetrate
the mortal veil:

> Men have I known and men, but never one
> Was grown so free an essence, or become
> So simply element as what I am.
> The mist goes from the mirror and I see.
> Behold! the world of forms is swept beneath—

The symbolist endeavor was based on a kind of alchemy of
words, and Pound thought of it in those terms. But Pound had
other interests as well, which would soon lead him to disassociate
himself from the symbolists. While he shared their concern with

the power of precise language to alter perception, and while he never ceased trying to see what Paracelsus had seen, he was more interested in the man having the vision than he was in the possibility of recreating that vision for the reader. The poem is only thirteen lines long, and little complexity is possible in so short a space. And yet when the poem's tone of calm wisdom is set beside the title, with its almost comic rhyme and the insertion of Paracelsus' name in a phrase customarily associated with God ("Gloria in excelsis Deo"), the impression created is that of a man who displays his self-importance with his wisdom: "Being no longer human, why should I/Pretend humanity or don the frail attire?" Pound was learning that no vision ever exists apart from the very particular qualities of the man or woman who dreams it.

IV   The Persona

Pound believed Browning's dramatic monologue to be the most interesting form in Victorian poetry, and he admired the older poet's concrete individuality of style. But Browning was only one of the precedents before Pound, and while some of Pound's poems are very much like dramatic monologues, none of them is wholly imitative of Browning, and many fall somewhere between the fully dramatic, and the simply personal, lyric. The situation surrounding the experience described in "The Tree," for instance, is just too slightly sketched to justify the term "dramatic," and yet that poem's exploration of emotion and point of view offers an important insight into why Pound was interested in the dramatic monologue. Writing to William Carlos Williams in 1908, he said: "To me the short so-called dramatic lyric—at any rate the sort of thing I do—is the poetic part of a drama the rest of which (to me the prose part) is left to the reader's imagination or implied or set in a short note. I catch the character I happen to be interested in at the moment he interests me, usually a moment of song, self-analysis, or sudden understanding or revelation. And the rest of the play would bore me and presumably the reader. I paint my man as I *conceive* him."[9] If the dramatic monologue's portrayal of specific character, concretely distinguished, interested him, it was only the subjective experience of that character, the emotion or the vision of a moment, which truly mattered. For Pound only this emotional "revelation" is poetic, while the dramatic context seems like prose, and therefore has no central place in the finished poem. Pound's emphasis is on the interesting *moment*, and *sudden* understanding, a concern which became central to imagist theory and the poetic practice of *The Cantos*. He distrusted the discursive moralizing of the major nineteenth-century English writers, and he found the similar working-out of a dramatic "argument" uninteresting. What he did value was the visionary moment of heightened perception, and in Browning's *Men and Women* he saw the possibility of locating that moment, so tenuous and vague in the poetry of the nineties, in a world of real people.

Of the poems which imitate Browning's model of the dramatic revelation of character more closely, "Cino" (*P*, 6) is a good beginning. Pound himself disparaged it for failing to delineate its hero's character sharply enough ("He might be anyone"),[10] and when "Cino" is contrasted with some other poems in the same manner, the criticism appears to be justified. But Cino da Pistoia is far more than a cardboard figure. A witty vagabond, lyrical and irreverent by turns, he has loved more than one woman, and when he hints that his lord is illegitimate, and that he could ruin him if he told all he knew, Cino reveals a background of sexual and political intrigue, and a depth of personal hatred, only partly suppressed by his light manner. But those aspects of Cino's "story" are never more than hints, and the poem restricts itself pretty much to "the poetic part" of the drama.

"Cino" is about a moment of change, a turning from city to open road; from a lord who has the power (rightly or not), to a life as unsponsored vagabond; from singing women to seeking new subjects. The emotions which fill that moment of turning range from veiled bitterness, to boisterous cynicism, to a quieter mood which is close to the heart of Pound's admiration for the troubadour poets. Cino's unconstant love may be the opposite of Dante's love for Beatrice, but for both poets, there is a progression from women, to song, to God as light. Against Dante's reverent quest, Cino's mocking seems like blasphemy. But he too is caught by the "allurement" of women's beauty, and in the simplicity of lines which contain none of the defensive posing of other stanzas ("Pollo Phoibee, old tin pan"), he reveals his understanding of how insubstantial are the mortal women he has loved:

> Eyes, dreams, lips, and the night goes.
> Being upon the road once more,
> They are not.

Cino's statement might be read as no more than the cynical belief of a man for whom women are forgotten as soon as they are left behind. But Pound was deeply interested in the notion of woman as the symbol of a reality beyond the material, associated with divinity, and finally imaginable only in images of light. In his studies of Provençal verse, he explored the theory that troubadour love poetry could be interpreted in symbolic terms such as these, and this conception of the troubadours does parallel Cino's desire to seek "the gardens of the sun" in the sky's light, after acknowledging the transitory nature of that love of woman which he had known in the past. By the time he published an essay on the subject ("Psychology and Troubadours," in 1912), Pound had refined his ideas considerably. The effect of "Cino," however, is not to illustrate a possible theory of symbolic love poetry, but to present the emotions of a man at one specific point in his life. T.S. Eliot's "The Love Song of J. Alfred Prufrock" has seemed the source of modern poetry's techniques for exploring the dynamics of psychic conflict, but in its precise orchestration of cynicism, wistfulness, anger, and joking, "Cino" captures the shape of a mind defending itself against loss, and justifying its necessary future. If Pound's essays explain the philosophy of light in Provençal love poetry, his poem explores its psychological origin, in the emotions one man might have known.

A more remarkable attempt to deal with emotions in conflict or crisis is "La Fraisne" (P, 4). As Pound explains in a note which accompanied the poem until about 1920, the action concerns a troubadour, Miraut de Garzelas, who "after the pains he bore a-loving Riels of Calidorn and that to none avail, ran mad in the forest."[11] The story, invented by Pound, has Miraut leave the human world, and in his mind, even human form, to live as a tree in the forest. Miraut is mad, and the poem's real interest is in how that madness is portrayed. But like "Cino," there is a continuity between the specific (and in this case, insane) notions of the poem's created character, and ideas which interested Pound generally, and which he examined in a number of other places. In his note, he describes a feeling of being "divided between myself corporal and a self aetherial," and refers to a mystical merger with the natural world, which brings great peace:

When the soul is exhausted of fire, then doth the spirit return unto its primal nature and there is upon it a peace great and of the woodland
"Magna pax et silvestris"

Then becometh it kin to the faun and the dryad, a woodland-dweller amid the rocks and streams.

He mentions the Book of the Dead, James of Basel, and Yeats' "Celtic Twilight," revealing the rather vague mixture of mysticism, Celticism, and symbolist poetry from which he was drawing his ideas. Essentially, it was another example of the late-romantic desire to transcend the limits of our mortal vision, but the specific form it takes here is significant. The movement is out of human form into tree, stone, and stream, and while the Celtic tradition of such metamorphoses may be Pound's source (along with Ovid), the unity of man and nature remained a tenet of his faith for the rest of his life. Nearly forty years later, when he was writing *The Pisan Cantos* in an American army prison camp, and facing madness, like Miraut, it was just this sense of merger with green nature that gave him peace.

As a portrayal of how the mind functions in its less rational moments, "La Fraisne" goes far deeper than "Cino." The poem is in Miraut's voice, and he begins calmly enough, offering some details of his former life, when he was a "gaunt, grave councillor," strong enough still to be admired by the young men for his swordplay. The tone is reflective and wise, and when he begins to speak of his present life he seems at first to be describing simply a growing understanding. But by the third stanza, a clear split has developed between the rational surface of his speech and its content, which is suddenly very strange:

> I have curled 'mid the boles of the ash wood,
> I have hidden my face where the oak
> Spread his leaves over me, and the yoke
> Of the old ways of man have I cast aside.

He speaks of his new bride, "that was a dog-wood tree some syne," and describes the peace he has found, even though he knows men think him mad. As he explains his new peace, the nature of his bride, and the folly of those who call him mad, he

begins to repeat himself until finally even the rational surface of
his speech disintegrates:

> Once when I was among the young men . . .
> And they said I was quite strong, among the young men.
> Once there was a woman . . .
> . . . but I forget . . . she was . . .
> . . . I hope she will not come again.
>
> . . . I do not remember. . . .
> I think she hurt me once, but . . .
> That was very long ago.
>
> I do not like to remember things anymore.

Miraut has formed the delusion that he has merged with nature
as a way of defending himself against the painful memory of his
human failures. He comes close to a moment of truthful self-
analysis, but when those painful memories threaten to hurt him
again, his train of recollection breaks up in confusion and
avoidance. In creating so accurate a picture of a mind caught
between the struggle for self-awareness, and the need to
preserve its own irrational defense mechanisms, Pound had
deepened the possibilities of the dramatic monologue for
offering insight into human psychology.

"La Fraisne" was not Pound's only treatment of madness at the
time. "Piere Vidal Old" (P, 30) also deals with the thoughts of a
man whose experience in love has made him mad. In contrast to
the flavor of Celtic nature magic which pervades "La Fraisne,"
however, the tone of "Piere Vidal Old" is more actively
dramatic, deriving from the traditional biography on which
Pound based his poem. According to the biography, which Pound
summarizes in his headnote to the poem, Vidal had run mad "as a
wolf, because of his love for Loba of Penautier." But the moment
which Pound chooses for the focus of his poem is long after the
event, consisting, like "La Fraisne," in the disturbed memories of
an old man. Less concerned in this poem to describe the conflict
of Vidal's mind, Pound emphasizes his vivid recollection of the
past. Only at the end does Pound attempt to mirror Vidal's
madness by creating disorder in the surface of his text. There,
Vidal seems to have an intense vision of the hills of Cabaret,
where he had run wild, followed suddenly by the disappearance

of whatever line had separated memory from delusion for him. He shouts at imaginary attackers and then sniffs the air, as a wolf again, and the poem's ending leaves him to his madness: "Ha! this scent is hot!" But for the most part, Pound's regular, rhymed stanzas do not attempt to suggest Vidal's madness through disordered form. There is a suggestion of too much intensity, amounting to obsession, in his attempt to justify his actions for those mockers who seem to him to be laughing at his foolishness. And the remembered joy of killing dog and deer with his own teeth does serve to undercut Vidal's claims for the worth of what he calls "that great madness." But the poem's chief concern is simply to recreate the emotions of a moment when the memory of a lover, the sorrow of her loss, long-nurtured anger at those who had shamed him, and a fanatical sense of his own rightness come together in Vidal's mind:

> Ah God, the Loba! and my only mate!
> Was there such flesh made ever and unmade!
> God curse the years that turn such women grey!
> Behold here Vidal, that was hunted, flayed,
> Shamed and yet bowed not and that won at last.

The effect is subtler than that created by the portrayal of obvious incoherence, and it indicates how far, even in 1908, Pound had been able to carry the lesson he had learned from Browning.

Given the project of making poems which reveal character by fixing on moments of intense emotion, however, men who have been made mad by grief or suffering are rather easy subjects. When Pound made tentative attempts to represent their madness by disordering a few lines of each poem, he was not attempting anything unprecedented (Shakespeare used the technique), but his experiments did anticipate the renewed romantic assumption, fundamental to twentieth-century free verse, that form and content are inseparable. But less extreme states of consciousness must be dealt with as well, and the technical problem which had to be solved in every poem, not just when special effects were needed, was how to make private experience clear without falling back on discursive generaliza-tion—Pound's main criticism of Browning. The only solution was to choose tone, syntax, diction, and image so precisely that the particulars of a personality would be embodied concretely, and the reader would have no need for the poet's guiding voice.

"Marvoil" (*P*, 22) is another poem based on Pound's study of the troubadours, but its hero, Arnaut of Marvoil, imagines himself to be neither wolf nor tree. He is simply a poet, suffering exile and the loss of his lady, through the jealousy of a rival, Alfonso of Aragon. But though he too suffers, he is fully in command of himself as he sits in an inn of Avignon, thinking of the countess of Beziers, writing a poem for her, and hiding it in a hole in the wall. No more successful than Vidal in keeping his lady, Marvoil nevertheless responds to his conventional situation not by the conventional love-madness, but by a witty, colloquial arrogance. The poem combines a testy personal note with all the intricate compliment of traditional Provençal love verse: for three stanzas Marvoil extends his image of the hole in the wall, which is hollow like his heart when the countess is not before him, which moans with a sound like sorrow when the wind blows across its emptiness, and which, like his heart, can hide the poem which bears his secret love. The chief accomplishment of "Marvoil," and of many of the poems which Pound modeled after Browning, is to have captured more than one aspect of a man's complexity in his speech. There is tenderness in Arnaut's reverie, and the tenderness changes easily into hatred for his rival; but the hatred is less bitter than simply wry, and hardly spoils the mood:

> May her eyes and her cheek be fair
> To all men except the King of Aragon,
> And may I come speedily to Beziers
> Whither my desire and my dream have preceded me.

When Pound's Arnaut addresses his hole in the wall he reveals himself as a man who is master of the conventions of his craft, but whose wit, and personal suffering, have combined to temper his reverence for those conventions. He writes his poem of love, but he defends himself from further hurt by a joke.

As Pound explored the notion of persona he gradually came to define for himself just what it was that seemed so wrong about the literature of the great Victorians. Against the sharp particularity of characters who had to be defined one from another, the discursiveness of Tennyson or Arnold seemed like a dull sermon. Pound distrusted their moral generalizing more and more, and he turned instead to the example of poets who had written about the specific tone of a personality, or the emotions of a single moment. He wanted to record experiences of "song, self-analysis, or sudden understanding," and to do so by choosing just the proper image, slangy insult, or pattern of rhythm. Though he could not name it yet, he was beginning to define the imagist doctrine.

CHAPTER 2

In Search of a Live Tradition

I   Patria Mia

IN his early experiments in imitation of Browning, Yeats, and the verse of the English decadents, Pound had been learning to shape his language with a craftsman's zeal which he first encountered in the poetic values of the Anglo-French symbolists. His academic studies in English and Romance literatures, and his early contact with Europe, and contemporary European writers, had led him to range widely through the verse of half a dozen languages in search of models for his own tentative skills. But his search was not simply a technician's shopping trip. Almost from the beginning, Pound's desire to build the mastery of his craft in a context defined by the greatest works of every accessible tradition was accompanied by a vision of the social usefulness of his endeavor. He was an American, and like other American writers before him, he was held by dreams of a new beginning. Responding to Harriet Monroe's invitation to contribute to her new magazine, *Poetry,* in 1912, Pound immediately outlined a program for revitalizing poetry in America, and he made his immodest goal quite clear: "Any agonizing that tends to hurry what I believe in the end to be inevitable, our American Risorgimento, is dear to me. That awakening will make the Italian Renaissance look like a tempest in a teapot! The force we have, and the impulse, but the guiding sense, the discrimination in applying the force, we must wait and strive for."[1] Like Harriet Monroe, Pound hoped to build an artistic movement capable of realizing the great natural "force" they both felt in their nation. But unlike her, Pound looked to a much more inclusive social, as well as artistic, renaissance, and he demanded a rigor of "discrimination" which might come from traditions older, and other, than America's. However much they shared a common goal, it was this conception of a cosmopolitan standard of craftsmanship brought to the service of a particular cultural program, which led to much of Pound's stormy relationship, during the next few years, with a magazine which truly desired an awakening of the arts in America, but which distrusted the influence of Europe.

In 1912 Pound began writing a series of articles for *The New Age* which were published together as *Patria Mia* in 1913. In those essays he sets down a great variety of thoughts about his nation, but his central thesis is that in spite of all its absurdities, "America has a chance for Renaissance."[2] *Patria Mia* is a fairly shapeless series of pronouncements on the state of America, combining the astute observation of particulars with an eager expectation of the millenium, and, as with so many American writers, a bitter note of disappointment which prefigures the increasing alienation of Pound's later years. But at the heart of his argument is the belief that America's new beginning must result from a gathering of all that is finest in the whole world's past.[3] For Pound, that belief meant that he must know literatures as various as those of classical Greece and Rome, and Provence and Tuscany in the Middle Ages, that he must know German lyrics and Renaissance English song. By 1914 he had added China and Egypt to his list.[4] What he sought of social justice, spiritual insight, and clarity of thought in those distant traditions only came together very gradually in his mind as a coherent vision of cultural unity. The desire to remake the country he had left was present very early in Pound's thought, and it drove him to search broadly for the roots of a whole society. But poetry was still the heart of it, and for the poet who would make vital use of foreign traditions, translation had to be among the first tasks: "A great age of literature is perhaps always a great age of translations; or follows it."[5]

II   The Seafarer

If there is any single key to Pound's greatness as a translator, it is in the fact that he never worked by simply taking the forms of English verse and filling them with the content of foreign poems. Hugh Kenner describes it this way: "Ezra Pound never translates 'into' something already existing in English. The Chinese or Greek or Provençal poem being by hypothesis something new, if it justifies the translator's or the reader's time, . . . something correspondingly new must be made to happen in English verse."[6] And Sister Bernetta Quinn has also described the crucial importance of Pound's belief that "the translator's work consists in causing a thing to recur in matter different from the original."[7]Although he gradually came to see a larger significance in this principle, Pound had begun with a particular insight into the possibilities of translation: any poem may be the concrete manifestation of a very complicated moment of thought, emotion and music; and if a poet would attempt translation, he must find a way to let that moment become manifest again, in new words.

Anglo-Saxon was not a major source for Pound, but he did find there an idiom with which to begin his *Cantos,* and the one full translation which does survive offers a very interesting insight into his techniques. *The Seafarer,* in Old English, was an elegiac poem told in the voice of a man whose life at sea leads him to the pain of loneliness and physical hardship. He yearns for the warm life of the landsman, and yet he is driven to the sea, which gradually takes on a symbolic quality as God's larger purpose is weighed against the very appealing, but transitory, springtime on land. The poem's attractiveness for Pound is easily understood: it offers a fascinating revelation of inner conflict in a tone which is both tough and sensitive, and supported by very specific detail. It could very easily be seen as dramatic monologue, but first Pound had to make it his own. His most significant change was simply to leave out the Christian material entirely, a decision which he justified in a note appended to the poem when it was published in *The New Age:*

Philological note: The text of this poem is rather confused. I have rejected half of line 76, read "Angles" for angels in line 78, and stopped translating before the passage about the soul and the longer lines beginning, "Mickle is the fear of the Almighty," and ending in a dignified but platitudinous address to the Deity: "World elder, eminent creator, in all ages, amen." There are many conjectures about how the text came into its present form. It seems most likely that a fragment of the original poem, clear through about the first thirty lines, and thereafter increasingly illegible, fell into the hands of a monk with literary ambitions, who filled in the gaps with his own guesses and "improvements." The groundwork may have been a longer narrative poem, but the "lyric," as I have accepted it, divides fairly well into "The Trials of the Sea," its Lure, and the Lament for Age.[8]

This note is a characteristic mixture of Pound's scholarly pretensions and personal prejudices. He had little sympathy for most of Christianity, and he was particularly interested in what he considered to be the persistence of pagan culture into the Christian Middle Ages. And in poetry, he distrusted all generalization and sermonizing, regarding such passages as no better than Tennysonian rhetoric. The result can be seen by comparing Pound's paganized version to this more literal translation:

> Wherefore each man should strive, before he leaves
> This world, to win the praise of those living
> After him. The best of posthumous fame
> Is to achieve great deeds on earth
> Against the malice of the fiends, against the devil,
> So that the children of men may honour a man's name
> And his fame at last may live with the angels
> For ever and ever, in the joy of life eternal
> Amongst the heavenly host.[9]

And here is Pound's version:

> And for this, every earl whatever, for those speaking after—
> Laud of the living, boasteth some last word,
> That he will work ere he pass onward,
> Frame on the fair earth 'gainst foes his malice,
> Daring ado, ...
> So that all men shall honour him after
> And his laud beyond them remain 'mid the English,
> Aye, for ever, a lasting life's-blast,
> Delight 'mid the doughty.

By rejecting, as corrupt, an embarrassing line about devils, and by reading "English" for the Anglo-Saxon "englum" (angels), Pound has made a pagan elegy in praise of fame gained through feats of arms, the only solace of the Germanic hero contemplating the loss of all his fellows. In his note he calls the poem a "lyric," distinguishing it from some larger narrative which may

have contained it, and his conception is still in keeping with the
purpose he defined in his letter of 1908 to William Carlos
Williams: to catch that moment of special awareness or emotion,
and leave the rest of the drama to a note or the reader's
imagination. For Pound's seafarer, the moment has been
transformed from a personal conflict between pagan feeling and
Christian vision into a purely pagan contemplation of time's
wastage: "Lordly men are to earth o'ergiven."

III   *Provence and the Troubadours*

Pound's richest mine of medieval lore and model, however,
was further south. He had begun his reading of the Troubadour
poets as an undergraduate, and by the time he came to London
he already regarded their work as offering an historical,
philosophical, and poetic example of major importance. Provençal literature contained much to interest him, and not least a
body of poetry already associated in medieval times with a
collection of vivid, romanticized lives of the poets. For the young
Pound, fascinated by the possibilities of dramatic lyric, there
seemed endless matter for drawing those intense moments of
character revealed. Bertran de Born, for example, provided
Pound with such a moment in "Sestina: Altaforte," a poem which
announced Pound's entrance into London's literary world in
startling terms, when he read it to T. E. Hulme's group in 1909.
As his understanding of Provençal and Tuscan thought continued
to grow and change in later years, Pound looked to the work of
other men. But Bertran was among his earliest interests, and as
late as 1915, with "Near Perigord," he was still the subject of a
major poem. His appeal, for a poet who had learned to draw his
characters after Browning, is obvious. Bertran was a twelfth-
century troubadour—a warrior, poet, lover, and a man placed in
hell by Dante, who labeled him "stirrer up of strife." Though
"Sestina: Altaforte" does reflect poems, or parts of poems, by
Bertran, it is not translation, but an imaginative exercise in
creating a persona, taking its direction from Dante's judgment
(quoted in the epigraph) and from those few fragments of
genuine translation. Filling his poem with images of violence, and
letting that bloody darkness color everything from music to the
weather, Pound creates a near maniac—exuberant, fascinating,
even persuasive—but obsessed by homicide. There is little

complexity in his character, but the sense of intense emotion, the cast of a mind at one moment of its life, is as powerful as anything he had yet attempted.

"Planh For the Young English King," however, also published in 1909, is an actual translation of a poem by Bertran, and its contrast with "Sestina" reveals a great deal about Pound's assumptions. The poem was a lament for the death of Prince Henry Plantagenet, eldest son of Henry II, who had aided Bertran in his own political struggles with the prince's brother, Richard Coeur de Lion. Although the "Planh" is a translation, it too defines its persona, in the Bertran who speaks his elegy. Unlike his bloodthirsty counterpart in "Sestina: Altaforte," this Bertran is sensitive and pious, suffering the loss of a beloved friend. Although his loss is also a political blow, there is no hint of that motive here, as Bertran describes a prince who was the earthly embodiment of all high virtue. In poems like "Cino" and the Villonauds, Pound, searching for a usable tradition, had very early been willing to reshape the past according to his own experience of the present. But he was also learning to move one step further—to understand that the past can be known only in these distorting and fragmentary ways. Many artists in the first decades of the twentieth century were coming to see their world as discontinuous, and limited by their own subjectivity. Pound never joined them fully in their growing sense of isolation. He wanted to know his world, present and past, and believed he could. But he also knew the lesson taught by writers like Browning and Henry James—that to draw a character from one specific point of view is to abandon the general, and to accept, at least in part, the limitations of subjectivity. Bertran de Born is a bloody warrior in one poem, while in another he becomes a man of deep sensitivity. Pound was exploring the history of his man, Bertran de Born, but even more important, he was exploring the nature of knowing itself.

To write two poems offering two distinct facets of a single reality, however, was not yet anything the nineteenth century had not achieved. It was only several years later that Pound caught up with the painters, who had already learned to begin the modernist movement by combining alternative points of view on a single canvas. What Pound had accomplished before 1910 was a very self-conscious sifting of certain times past, an attempt to learn how imagination may act to shape our record of lives once lived in fact. The clearest example of that effort, with regard to Bertran de Born, may be found in two poems— "Dompna Pois de me No'us Cal" and "Na Audiart"—the first a translation, the second Pound's fictive variation by means of persona, on the same theme. The original poem involves Bertran's creation of a "borrowed lady," as he combines the best features of a number of real ladies into an imagined figure who must console him for the loss of his mistress. In "Na Audiart," Pound has him addressing his poem, not to his beloved, Maent, but to Audiart, who had contributed "the lineaments of the torse" to his ideal lady. Far more complex than the personae of either the "Planh" or "Sestina: Altaforte," this Bertran is a lover whose speech is graceful, ironic, and slyly lascivious. The poem's dramatic occasion is Audiart's hostility, and the response which Bertran makes to it. And Pound has caught a tone which is remarkably subtle in its use of conventional literary praise to express contradictory feelings. Bertran is teasingly seductive in his compliment ("'Cause never a flaw was there/Where thy torse and limbs are met"), focusing his praise on the attractiveness of her body. And yet a deeper level of hostility is revealed when he moves on—still in very conventional terms—to consider the mortal decay which that body's beauty must know eventually. There is no hint of the theme of mortality in the original poem, but by inserting it into his own version, Pound is able to portray the complexity of feeling in a man who can mock a woman's disdain in the very terms with which he seems to praise her.

Pound had been familiar with Bertran's "Dompna Pois" very early, translating some of it by 1908, although the final version was not published until 1914. It would be nearly impossible to distinguish the stages of Pound's thought, as they remain in the finished poem. But the "Dompna Pois" which interested him enough to publish it six years after "Na Audiart," speaks with a very different voice. There is much less drama, or sense of emotion sharpened to do hurt. The poem seems more conventional, duller, and yet Pound has once again altered his model in ways distinctively his own. Bertran addresses Maent rather simply, explaining his scheme to make a borrowed lady, "since you care nothing for me." He ranges among his ladies, "culling from each a fair trait," but when he has finished, his creation is something more than just fine throat and hair and stature. As Stuart McDougal has pointed out,[10] Pound has not created the borrowed lady of the original poem, but a "phantom," idealized and ethereal, where the Provençal is simply carnal. There is passion in his "flame-lap," to be sure, but the spiritual quality has come to be at least as important. If the characterization in "Na Audiart" emphasizes a dramatic situation and complex emotions, the conception of Bertran in this poem is more intellectualized, moving in the direction of a private, symbolic, and spiritual experience. As Pound learned more about the culture of medieval Provence, his interest shifted in just this way, from fascination with the lives, to greater concern for the symbolic meaning of the verse.

IV   *"Psychology and Troubadours"*

Soon after Pound's arrival in London in 1908, he was offered the chance to deliver a series of lectures at the London Polytechnic. The Series, on "The Development of Literature in Southern Europe," took place early in 1909, and it was followed in the fall by an expanded series running on through the winter of 1910. The lectures were published in that year as *The Spirit of Romance,* Pound's first full volume of prose. They contain many early experiments in translation, and they offer good insight into the technical interest which this verse held for him as he sought to expand and perfect the mastery of his craft. And while some of his analysis is simply the remainder of graduate school research, much is extremely significant for its record of his developing thought. Among the arguments which he tested for the first time in *The Spirit of Romance* were ideas which became central to all the rest of his creative work.

Pound's interest in history, and his own strong sense of social right and wrong, had early led him to see cultural change in terms of value judgments, and nowhere is that predisposition clearer than in his study of the Middle Ages. In a chapter on Villon, for example, he makes a distinction between medieval and Renaissance culture in terms of architectural design. Medieval work valued the structure of line and composition, whereas later architects were enamored of sheer mass: "The Gothic architect envied the spider his cobweb. The Renaissance architect sought to rival the mountain. They raised successively the temple of the spirit and the temple of the body."[11] Pound saw the history of our art after the Middle Ages as largely a decline into matter—the depiction of "meat" in painting and the admiration of mass in building. There were exceptions to the general decadence, of course, such as the Elizabethan song lyric, but for the most part later artists seemed to have lost that vision which so distinguished the Middle Ages: the perception of a beauty and meaning beyond the mundane, a sense of formal structure (Gothic architecture) or symbolic image (Dante's light) capable of leading us to the apprehension of a reality hidden from normal vision. That Pound would find such a quality in the imaginative life of the Middle Ages is not terribly surprising, given his early enthusiasm for symbolist poetry, which also sought a language of art designed to evoke the invisible. When he found Provence, it seemed to confirm his hope that a way of being treasured in his own time by only a few men and women, in the face of exile and public scorn, had once been the way of a whole culture.

The most interesting chapter in *The Spirit of Romance*, however, was not originally a part of that book at all. Entitled "Psychology and Troubadours," it was published as an article in 1912 in *The Quest*, a journal devoted to the study of mysticism and the occult, and only in 1932 was it made a chapter of the book. In it, Pound develops a theory which supports his perception of the visionary strain in medieval verse. His central thesis is that a "visionary interpretation" of Provençal poetry may be made. He suggests that the symbolic language of such poetry represents a religious tradition older than Christian Europe, that a spirit of Hellenic paganism may have survived, in Provence, the Northern invasions of the "darker ages."[12] The result, in Pound's view, was an "unofficial mysticism," a visionary cult made out of half-remembered details of the pagan mysteries, restless seeking of the troubadours, and the experience of human love. Their cult found its expression in a poetry which Pound defended against the charge of obscurity: as a "ritual" intended to reveal its special knowledge "to those who are already expert," this poetry should be distinguished from the simpler poetry of lyric song, which was also valuable, in its own way. In making such a distinction, Pound was defining the course of his own future work, which would take the verbal difficulty and the evocation of personal vision from the symbolists, but without the more strictly private tendencies of their verse. *The Cantos*, like the poetry of Pound's imagined troubadours, is a

visionary poetry intended to communicate with its audience,
even if that audience must already be, to some extent, initiated.

In speculating about the possibility of such a cult among the
troubadours, Pound had begun to articulate a theory of knowing
which soon became central to his own poetics. He questioned the
"mediumistic properties" of chivalric love: "Stimulated by the
color or quality of emotion, did that 'color' take on forms
interpretive of the divine order? Did it lead to an 'exteriorization
of the sensibility,' and interpretation of the cosmos by feeling?"[13]
Pound is speaking here of knowledge, of insight into the deepest
nature of the world. But he conceives that knowledge to be
available not through logic and reason, but through "feeling,"
through a capacity to render emotion manifest in language, and
to read there an order which transcends the human. Referring to
the troubadours as an "aristocracy of emotion," Pound is entirely
serious in his attempt to build a theory of knowledge on this
nonrational basis. In such early poems as "The Tree," he had
described moments of intense *experience* as leading to new
understanding, and by 1912, in his explorations of Provençal
verse, he had begun to define consciously what had long been
merely implicit assumptions in his poetic practice. Such
knowledge as he imagined the troubadours to possess would
have come through images charged with symbolic meaning—and
read whole, in moments of sudden illumination—not through the
progressive steps of discursive argument.

Pound had discovered (or invented) a theory of knowledge
implicit in Provençal verse which he was soon to incorporate into
the aesthetic rationale of his own developing modernism. But the
implications of his "Psychology and Troubadours" are wider still.
If emotion may be read as an "interpretation of the cosmos,"
then its basis must not be simply personal and transitory.
Discussing Greek myth, Pound suggests that it "arose when
someone having passed through delightful psychic experience
tried to communicate it to others and found it necessary to
screen himself from persecution." The myths thus become
"explications of mood," but Pound's qualification is crucial: "Our
kinship to the ox we have constantly thrust upon us; but beneath
this is our kinship to the vital universe, to the tree and the living
rock, and, because this is less obvious—and possibly more
interesting—we forget it." For Pound, man is part of a living
universe, and that fact is fundamental to poetry and myth alike:

As to his consciousness, the consciousness of some seems to rest, or to have its center more properly, in what the Greek psychologists called the *phantastikon*. Their minds are, that is, circumvolved about them like soap-bubbles reflecting sundry patches of the macrocosmos. And with certain others their consciousness is "germinal." Their thoughts are in them as the thought of the tree is in the seed, or in the grass, or the grain, or the blossom. And these minds are the more poetic, and they affect mind about them, and transmute it as the seed the earth. And this latter sort of mind is close on the vital universe; and the strength of the Greek beauty rests in this, that it is ever at the interpretation of this vital universe, by its signs of gods and godly attendants and oreads.[14]

Not only is man always a part of his living world, but some men are possessed by a quality of mind which enables them to go beyond that simple participation, to *interpret* the vital universe, and then to pass that insight on to others. In his metaphoric description of such minds as "germinal," as transmuting mind around them just as seeds cause the earth to bloom, Pound had formulated his lifelong faith in the interrelationship of divine order, living nature, human experience, and poetic word. Through images which succeed in articulating his own emotion, the poet can reveal those deeper levels of order from which his own feeling springs.

Although much of his later philosophy was beginning to find a shape in the speculations of *The Spirit of Romance* and "Psychology and Troubadours," Pound's work during those years was still very much a combination of the old and the new. In 1911, for example, he published *Canzoni of Ezra Pound*, a volume which contained poems such as "Erat Hora," "Ballatetta," and "The Altar"—still heavily influenced by nineteenth-century aesthetics. Two clear examples of Pound's gradual accommodation of new and old in that volume are "The Flame" and "The House of Splendour." "The Flame" is about the poet's endeavor to transcend the limits of the mundane. Pound loads the poem with all the trappings of Celtic twilight and Pre-Raphaelite image (Oisin's tales, rare jewels, the "shadow of a darkling world," etc.) and his poet's visionary experience, on regarding the beauty of Lake Garda, could be that of any romantic nature poet. Although the poem opens with a reference to Pound's belief in the visionary wisdom of Troubadour poetry (" 'Tis not a game of barter, lands and houses,/Provence knew"), the effect is to make clear how great the continuity was between his earliest poetic values, derived from Rossetti and the nineties, and the evolving theories of poetry and knowledge which would eventually become the basis for his radically innovative new poetry.

Similarly, "The House of Splendour" suggests the theories of Provençal verse which Pound was formulating at the time, and yet dresses those theories in the conventions of the nineties. In "Psychology and Troubadours," Pound notes Richard St. Victor's notion that some trace of the ineffable splendors of paradise may be recalled by naming all the beautiful things we have seen, and he suggests that the troubadour, "either more indolent or more logical," simply condensed all those images of beauty into the single image of his Lady, who then became a kind of *mantram*. "The House of Splendour," for all its Pre-Raphaelite atmosphere, portrays just such an experience:

> And I have seen my Lady in the sun,
> Her hair was spread about, a sheaf of wings.
> And red the sunlight was, behind it all.

The Lady inhabits "a house not made with hands," and the poet's experience is clearly one of transcendent vision—to "Break down the four-square walls of standing time"—a mystical program which hinges on the symbolic power of the Lady he beholds. Early in his career, Pound had been attracted by the sound of such poetry, and when his study of the troubadours seemed to reveal a poetic practice which had served spiritual meaning, as well as song, his natural response was to bring Provençal and symbolist visions together. When he did so, he found a congruence which taught him yet another crucial lesson: that a world which had once been, might be again.

V *Tuscan Poetry*

The Provençal culture which Pound had found so illuminating came to an end in the early part of the thirteenth century, when a papal crusade was launched against the Albigensian heretics whose stronghold was Provence. Pound saw in that crusade an orthodox hatred for the Provençal "servants of Amor," and he also suggested an economic motive which anticipates some of his later concerns. [15] Whatever the cause, when Provençal power was broken, the vitality of its culture also failed, and new achievement in poetry moved south, to the poets of Tuscany. The transition seemed a natural one to Pound, as the mystical Lady of the troubadours was adopted by the Italian poets, there to be elaborated into a more complex and intellectual symbolism.

Pound had been familiar with the Tuscan poets for a number of years, and his interest in the visionary symbol of the Lady had in fact been awakened by their work. In 1910 he wrote an introduction to the poetry of Cavalcanti, which he had translated, for a volume eventually to be published in 1912 as the *Sonnets and Ballate of Guido Cavalcanti*. In his introduction, he describes the "spiritual chemistry" of Guido's world, and particularly the concept of *virtù* ("the efficient property of a substance or person") which may be visible, symbolically, to the poet who regards his Lady: "thou shall see depart from her lips her subtler body, and from that a still subtler form ascends and from that a star, the body of pure flame surrounding the source of the *virtù*, which will declare its nature." [16] This notion of light, emanating from the Lady and serving to manifest her special virtue, as shaped by the stars, was especially meaningful to Pound, and he used it in a variety of ways. In "Ballatetta," for example, published in 1909, Pound echoes Cavalcanti in a brief poem which takes the Lady's light for subject. The speaker's heart (in a line out of Cavalcanti) is in the Lady's "jurisdiction," but the poem is less concerned with his love than with the nature of her light, which is her essence spun out to "gossamer" thinness. The light clearly transcends our human limits, as it parches grass, and makes ordinary mortals seem nothing more than shadows shaped to human form. "Ballatetta" is a slight poem, as its title suggests. But while it attempts little beyond the statement of a few beautiful images, it does serve as yet another example of Pound's early readiness to write a visionary poetry.

The foremost medieval lady who led her poet to see the light of a higher world was, of course, Dante's Beatrice. Dante had described his first vision of Beatrice in the *Vita Nuova*, and Pound's "Apparuit" (1912) is based on that description. In characteristic fashion, Pound ignores the drama and focuses on just that moment of awed discovery and intense emotion when Dante first glimpses his beloved:

> Crimson, frosty with dew, the roses bend where
> thou afar, moving in the glamorous sun,
> drinkst in life of earth, of the air, the tissue
> golden about thee.

The speaker is stunned to perceive this girl, "a slight thing," assuming so marvelous an aura, appearing to him as a "portent." She seems to have cast loose "the cloak of the body," and her appearance evokes a transcendent reality, represented by pervasive images of light. Her throat is "aflash with strands of light inwoven about it," and she is clothed in "goldish weft" which is so insubstantial as to seem the work of "magical hands." As an exploration of Dante's symbolic world, the poem is typical of Pound's way of knowing. Avoiding a narrative or philosophical approach, Pound examines his subject through the lens of the dramatic lyric. In limiting his poem to the intense emotion of a single moment's experience, he was choosing a way which seemed truer than the historian's generalization, and more interesting than a story.

As Pound's interests broadened in succeeding years, he continued to draw on his early studies of Provençal and Tuscan verse, and particularly on the idealized love which he had encountered there. Whether translating or fashioning new poems in homage to the old, Pound refined his ideas as he progressed in the mastery of his craft. "The Alchemist," published in 1920, was an original poem, but it builds on Pound's assertion of 1910, in the introduction to his *Cavalcanti*, that "the equations of alchemy were apt to be written as women's names and the women so named endowed with the magical powers of the compounds."[17] The poem, subtitled "Chant for the Transmutation of Metals," is an attempt to conjure by the ritual repetition of women's names, chosen for their beautiful sound. Although Pound has added the alchemical desire to change base metal into gold, the poem's primary subject is still that light—now the light of gold—which is symbolic evidence of the mystical Lady's unique power. As his remarks in the *Cavalcanti* introduction make clear, Pound understood that alchemy was not simply a medieval get-rich-quick scheme, but a serious endeavor of science, philosophy, and mysticism. Gold is like the sun, and the sun is like God. To ascend in vision is to attain a higher wisdom, a more refined humanity, and it is through the image of woman, surrounded by a light which links her with heaven, that the way of ascent may be learned.

If this vision seems to constitute a Platonic yearning for some transcendent reality, however, it is a yearning which in no way depends on a rejection of the natural world. For Pound, the troubadours were "opposed to a form of stupidity not limited to Europe, that is, idiotic asceticism and a belief that the body is evil."[18] In "Terra Italica," an essay published in 1931, Pound expanded his earlier theory of pagan survivals in Provençal culture, arguing particularly that the cult of Eleusis had persisted there, though rejected elsewhere by the Christian church. He believed that the Eleusinian mysteries had con-tributed an "inextinguishable source of beauty" to Provençal song, and that they had acted as "the strongest counter force to the cult of Atys and asceticism."[19] Pound rejects the charge, made at the time of the Albigensian Crusade, that Provence harbored a Manichean heresy, arguing instead that if any unorthodox belief existed it was Eleusinian, and not that Manichean distrust of the material world. And he argued that "at the root of any mystery" must lie a "consciousness of the unity with nature." Such a consciousness could hardly be reconciled with the ascetic perception of nature as evil, as wholly separate from the Divine.

This sense of our human continuity with the natural world was central to Pound's own belief, and the imagery of "The Alchemist" is filled with it. As he had written in "Psychology and Troubadours," Pound conceived of our lives as part of a continuous fabric of nature—living, flowing, changing. Light is literally the "power of grass," and from its white emergence in the seed to its fading in the copper and bronze of autumn leaves, light is the force which flows through every living thing. In the bright aura surrounding the Lady, expressing her essence and leading upward to heaven, the unity of tree, fish, woman, star, and God is made visible. And once visible, symbolically, its truth can be manifest in word, or poem, or alchemist's chant.

VI   "Provincia Deserta"

Pound's search among dead ages was not the pastime of a dilettante or a pedant. He was struggling to build a craft, an understanding of history, and increasingly, a better way to live in human society. He admired the technical integrity of the troubadour poets, and from them he learned to accommodate his early infatuation with Pre-Raphaelite symbolic ladies to a deeper and more inclusive meaning. Rejecting asceticism, he found in Provençal culture a way which valued both the body and its animating spirit: "The conception of the body as perfect instrument of the increasing intelligence pervades. The lack of this concept invalidates the whole of monastic thought."[20] But that balance of divine light against earthly matter was delicate, and with the end of the Middle Ages the danger came not from too much spirit, but too much flesh: European painting became more interested in "the dinner scene," and less in portraying "the body of air clothed in the body of fire."[21] Pound was interested in history only if he thought it could be of use to the present. His Provence had seemed to possess an order worth recreating, but that order had ended in Renaissance flesh, a fact which had to be understood before the Provence that was gone could be made new.

In 1913, Pound wrote an essay entitled "Troubadours—Their Sorts and Conditions," in which he discussed his own approach to Provence: "If a man of our time be so crotchety as to wish emotional, as well as intellectual, acquaintance with an age so out of fashion as the twelfth century, he may try in several ways to attain it."[22] The present, seemingly content to know the intellectual facts of history, made little effort to imagine the wholeness of life in an older age. But Pound was the poet who had begun with Browning, and his history was the record of moments. He knew that no pattern of a former time could ever be made to live again unless we could be shown feeling as well as fact. He suggested that we might read the old books, and see troubadour costumes in their illuminated capitals, listen to the music of the songs ("a little Oriental in feeling"), and even "walk the hill roads and river roads from Limoges and Charente to Dordogne and Narbonne and learn a little, or more than a little, of what the country meant to the wandering singers." The physical location of castles in a time of constant struggle, and even the weather, were part of the reality which the troubadours lived.

Pound had walked those roads himself, and when he married Dorothy Shakespear in 1914, they planned to make another walking tour of Provence, though World War I delayed their trip until 1919.[23] In 1915, however, he published a poem which deals with such a tour, and with the imaginative reconstruction of the past which gradually takes shape in the walker's mind. "Provincia Deserta" begins as a straightforward poem of description and reflection, told in the voice of a modern man. Pound describes the roads and river valleys, and the detailed texture of the place—trees "gray with lichen," a "pleached arbor," a "stream full of lillies." He pokes among old rafters, meets a garrulous old man at an inn, and notes the direction of the roads. And suddenly the clear line between modern observer and the past he imagines begins to blur. Climbing old stairs, and naming the castles of the troubadours, the past becomes vividly alive for the poem's speaker, who imagines the intense moments of life and death associated with each place. Beginning with brief, fragmentary recollections ("Here Coeur-de-Lion was slain/Here was good singing"), the poem builds to a fuller evocation of one particular drama concerning Pieire de Maensac, who had become a troubadour after flipping a coin with his brother to determine who would take their castle, and who go on the road. Pieire used his song to win a lady away from her husband, and with the Dauphin's protection, to keep her. Anticipating a technique which became central to *The Cantos*, Pound regards their story of stolen wife and angry husband as a "second Troy," a new instance of old pattern. Throughout the poem, however, he keeps a double perspective, with the imagined past set against a speaker who clearly lives in a later age. In the midst of lines which describe Provence living, he notes that Arles is now "greatly altered," and Dorata "ruined." The poem ends on this note of change:

> So ends that story.
> That age is gone;
> Pieire de Maensac is gone.
> I have walked over these roads;
> I have thought of them living.

Pound had discovered in the work of the troubadours a culture which valued body and spirit jointly, regarding man as part of a vast, interconnecting cosmos extending from nature to God and animated by a force described symbolically as light. That vision had been preserved in a poetic tradition which might be made to live again, but not by ignoring the present. "Provincia Deserta" builds on an understanding which Pound had acquired by 1912: that however beautiful Provence might be when seen through the lens of Rossetti and the nineties, it could not be a romantic image out of the nineteenth century, if it would serve the twentieth. Those lost visions might be wholly valid, but offered as matter of a worn-out age, they were invisible. Pound's task was to make his language new.

CHAPTER 3

Imagism and Vorticism

I   Toward a New Language

EARLY in his career, Pound had turned away from Victorian verse, which seemed to him too rhetorical, too much given to generalization, and too moralistic. He had looked instead to symbolist and decadent poetry, so thoroughly opposed to that public, discursive stance of the Victorians, and the example of writers like Swinburne, Rossetti, Johnson, Symons, and Yeats had served him well. Pound's own interests in private emotion and visionary ways of knowing drew him strongly to their work, and made it very difficult for him to see that they too were part of the past. They were, however, and by 1912 Pound could say as much in his essays. His realization came slowly, and partially, though some critics have seen its beginning—at least intuitively—quite early: "Pound was trying to grow out of a subjective generation which cultivated an inarticulate *Schwärmerei*. Like the Buddha's followers, he realized that the ego is the great hindrance to perception. So he tried to discipline his 'I' by making it an 'eye,' and chose the form of the *persona*—or mask—in which to cast much of his poetry."[1] The persona form did serve to distance the poem from its author. But if it was also Pound's first attempt to distance himself from the previous generation, it was doomed by its own medium—a language fashioned by the nineties. In poems like "Praise of Ysolt," "Famam Librosque Cano," "The White Stag," "The Eyes"—fully realized dramatic lyrics, or simple fragments—the language is built out of archaic words, languid rhythms, and romantically beautiful images. As "flame paleth," and deer leap " 'mid the clouds on the heather," and the poet protests that he is "worn

54

with travail," the impression of a fin-de-siècle indulgence in beautiful old things is strong indeed.

It was a way to begin, but Pound was gradually moving on, into his own century. He offered one version of how his enlighten-ment had begun in a 1939 obituary for the novelist, Ford Maddox Ford. Upon reading Pound's third volume of poetry, Ford had literally rolled on the floor in derision at Pound's attempts to master "the stilted language that then passed for 'good English.' "[2] Their meeting had taken place in 1911, shortly after the publication of *Canzoni*, a volume which, in poems such as "The Altar," "Erat Hora," and "The House of Splendour," had brought Pound's first poetic interests to a kind of culmination— or, as he later thought, dead end. Ford's influence was great, partly for the example he set of a sheer integrity of craft. In Ford's insistence that a "natural language" must be found, and in the quality of his own work, Pound learned a lesson which was made all the more impressive by Ford's personal aura of authority. And when he discovered the clean precision of Gustave Flaubert's language the following year, Pound's dis-enchantment with the mannered richness of his own previous style was confirmed.

When Pound reflected, in 1931, on his early attempts at translation, he saw that the state of his own language had been the greatest hindrance: "What obfuscated me was not the Italian but the crust of dead English, the sediment present in my own available vocabulary—which I, let us hope, got rid of a few years later."[3] He saw the education of a poet as necessarily a long process, in which the literature of the past must first be learned, and then escaped. At the heart of the process was the unavoidable fact that language is constantly changing, and that poets must change with it: "Neither can anyone learn English, one can only learn a series of Englishes. Rossetti made his own language. I hadn't in 1910 made a language, I don't mean a language to use, but even a language to think in." The Pound of 1931, and *The Cantos*, knew what he had only begun to guess in 1911: that the shape of language is not mere fashion, but a part of how we think. To change the forms of language is to change one fundamental way of knowing the world.

Within a few months of his encounter with Ford, Pound published a poem which indicates the direction his work was about to take. "The Return" is a poem about the forgotten gods and goddesses of a pagan age, and its style is direct and simple. To be sure, the subject is still that moment of special vision which had occupied so many of Pound's earlier poems, and the gods are "pallid" and dreamlike. But Pound never ceased to be a visionary, even after fifty years of *Cantos*, and his break with the poetic tradition of the immediate past was not so much one of content as of style. "The Return" avoids archaic diction and inverted word order, proceeding through a relatively simple elaboration of two grammatical structures: "See . . ." (movements, feet, trouble, etc.), and "These were . . ." (Gods, the keen-scented, etc.). The language is precise and restrained, creating an impression which Pound himself described two years later by comparing it to modern sculpture.[4]

Although he yields to capitalized abstraction briefly (" 'Wing'd-with-Awe'/Inviolable"), Pound creates his effect in this poem primarily through the careful presentation of details: a slow, troubled pace, a wavering movement, dogs "slow on the leash" where formerly they had been keen-scented, "sniffing the trace of air." The experience of the gods returning, dazed and wondering, into an unfamiliar world, is defined most clearly by concrete perceptions such as these, rather than by general statement. And while the technique is still rather tentative in "The Return," it anticipates some of the central assumptions of Pound's mature work. In 1911 and 1912, Pound published a series of articles in *The New Age* entitled "I Gather the Limbs of Osiris." Characteristically, the articles are a rather rambling series of observations about culture, history, and literature, but they offer good insight into his current attempt to forge a method of thought, as well as a style. Speaking of a "New Method in Scholarship," he defines what he calls "the method of Luminous Detail," distinguishing it from the prevailing mode of "multitudinous detail," and from "the method of sentiment and generalization" which had hindered a previous generation. His "luminous detail" is a very far-reaching concept: "Any fact is, in a sense, 'significant.' Any fact may be 'symptomatic,' but certain facts give one a sudden insight into circumjacent conditions, into their causes, their effects, into sequence, and law."[5] As early as "The Tree," of course, Pound had written about those particular, intense moments of experience which change our understanding of the world. But now he could extend that early notion into a kind of philosophy of knowledge: certain facts are capable of providing an insight which is "sudden" and visionary, rather than the result of a logical progression, which is nevertheless not a mere subjective impression. In Pound's assertion, cause and effect, and even "law" can be revealed at those moments when we suddenly apprehend the significance of certain crucial facts. Carefully selected, such facts can serve to interpret "the development of civilization or of literature": "A few dozen facts of this nature give us intelligence of a period—a kind of intelligence not to be gathered from a great array of facts of the other sort. These facts are hard to find. They are swift and easy of transmission. They govern knowledge as the switchboard governs an electric circuit."

In moving from the uniqueness of a knowledge gained in private experience, which he had described in poems like "The Tree," to an assertion that the complexity of history might also be understood through the perception of significant details, Pound was making a very large jump. In one sense, he was simply acting on the distrust he had always felt for the easy, distorting generalizations of the nineteenth century. Pound believed that such powerful details really do exist, objectively, amid the vast data of history or literature, and that to show them clearly, rather than blur them with generalization, was our greatest need. As his switchboard metaphor indicates, he saw the luminous detail as primarily a key to understanding, and therefore to communication, and he drew the obvious conclusion for art: "The artist seeks out the luminous detail and presents it. He does not comment. His work remains the permanent basis of psychology and metaphysics. Each historian will 'have ideas'— presumably different from other historians—imperfect inductions, varying as the fashions, but the luminous details remain unaltered." Pound is not simply describing the traditional practice of supporting a poem's argument with carefully chosen symbols and metaphors. The power of luminous detail to explain and enlighten on its own terms must be trusted, and in his statement that the artist "does not comment," Pound anticipates the radical innovations in poetic form which he was about to begin.

II *Imagism*

In 1912 Pound published a new volume of poetry, entitled *Ripostes*. It included "The Complete Poetical Works of T. E. Hulme"—five very brief poems—and a prefatory note by Pound,

who had met Hulme in 1909. At that time Hulme had been the
leader of a small group of poets disenchanted with the present
course of English poetry, and in his note Pound calls them a
"School of Images," and suggests that their work was "sounder"
than that of "the Impressionists who brought forth: 'Pink pigs
blossoming upon the hill-side;' or of the Post-Impressionists who
beseech their ladies to let down slate-blue hair over their
raspberry-coloured flanks" (P, 251). Rather enigmatically, Pound
suggests that those older follies are about to be attacked by a
new movement, which he names for the first time: "As for the
future, *Les Imagistes,* the descendents of the forgotten school of
1909, have that in their keeping." In August of 1912 Harriet
Monroe wrote to Pound from Chicago, asking him to contribute
to her new magazine, *Poetry.* He accepted, and in his
correspondence with her immediately began to make casual
references to his new school, calling one of his own poems "an
over-elaborate post-Browning 'Imagiste' affair," and then in
October sending in some poems of H. D. (which he signed "H.D.,
Imagiste") with a cover letter in which he called them "some
modern stuff by an American, I say modern, for it is in the laconic
speech of the Imagistes, even if the subject is classic."[6]

However casually it may have begun, imagism soon seemed to
be a viable new movement, and Pound began to think about
making its theoretical assumptions clearer. His own account of
how the movement had begun describes its first doctrine:

In the spring or early summer of 1912, "H.D.," Richard Aldington and
myself decided that we were agreed upon the three principles
following:

    1. Direct treatment of the "thing" whether subjective or objective.
    2. To use absolutely no word that does not contribute to the
presentation.
    3. As regarding rhythm: to compose in the sequence of the musical
phrase, not in sequence of a metronome.[7]

These rather general points of agreement summarize much of
Pound's earlier rejection of the elaborately conventional,
discursive quality of nineteenth-century verse. They emphasize
a concrete, economical use of language, and the avoidance of any
artificiality, whether of metrical scheme or rhetorical stance.

By early 1913, Pound had begun to formulate his imagist

program more fully, in "A Few Don'ts by an Imagist," published in *Poetry* magazine. Most significant was his definition of the image: "An 'Image' is that which presents an intellectual and emotional complex in an instant of time."[8] Invoking the authority of "the newer psychologists," he had found in "complex" a word which could name precisely the notion he had attempted to explain in his earlier discussion of luminous detail. The properly chosen image must communicate intellectual meaning as well as emotional force, and it must do so instantaneously. When he describes how such an image might be received, he uses terms which continue to suggest the visionary: "It is the presentation of such a 'complex' instantaneously which gives that sense of sudden liberation; that sense of freedom from time limits and space limits; that sense of sudden growth, which we experience in the presence of the greatest works of art." Pound had begun his career in the shadow of the symbolists, with their yearning to transcend the limits of the mundane world by attaining to a vision of unearthly beauty, and their influence was still present in this statement of 1913. The surface resemblance, however, is misleading, and in fact Pound's thought had by this time led him to a position which was opposed to symbolist theory in many ways. If the apprehension of Pound's image was an irrational experience, involving a sudden exhilarating sense of "liberation," it was nevertheless directed toward the real world, and it could issue in knowledge of political history or economics as easily as it could in visions of gods and goddesses. He argued that "the proper and perfect symbol is the natural object," and that the symbolic function must not dominate a poem to the exclusion of all other possible readings—including the literal.

Pound had learned point-of-view from Henry James and from Browning, and his explorations of the persona form had taught him much about the limits of subjectivity. For many artists of Pound's time, the symbolists, and the romantics before them, had expressed a sense of personal isolation, of doubt about the capacity of our limited senses to know anything objectively. Their skepticism was part of a general movement of Western thought toward ever increasing doubt about the foundations of knowledge and even the existence of a world outside ourselves. In the twentieth century, that current continued on to the existential doubt of Pirandello and Beckett, but for Pound the understanding of subjectivity was balanced by a counter faith in the objectivity of the world we touch and in our own capacity to know truly. In 1921 he addressed this problem directly in an essay called "Axiomata," in which he summarized a number of the most basic tenets of his belief. Affirming that "the intimate essence of the universe" (which he calls God) is "*not* of the same nature as our own consciousness," and that our consciousness could not have produced the universe, he concludes that God exists. But while our consciousness is in no way capable of understanding this essence, or *Theos,* it does not follow, for Pound, that the universe must remain a mystery: "The universe exists. By exists we mean normally: is perceptible to our consciousness or deducible by human reason from data perceptible to our senses."[9] Pound's response is not that of the simple realist who supposes he can refute the philosophical doubt of three hundred years by kicking a stone in the road. He acknowledges the validity of Dante's mysticism and his own poems are filled with the visionary. But he also insists that our world can be known, and in doing so he defines the uniqueness of his own position. Sharing the assumptions of many of the "avant-garde" about the limitations imposed by each individual's point of view, he did not carry those assumptions to the essentially conservative conclusions which reached their peak in absurdist drama: that human consciousness is private and unique, capable of knowing nothing beyond its own experience, and therefore capable of changing nothing in that larger world. Pound was a social activist who believed that the past could be known and the present changed by men and women whose consciousness, though strictly finite, was rooted in a continuous, living universe. To see the world concretely was the first step.

III   Ripostes

As Pound weighed the poetry of the recent past against that of the Middle Ages, and planned for the future, he concluded that, "in the art of Daniel and Cavalcanti, I have seen that precision which I miss in the Victorians, that explicit rendering, be it of external nature, or of emotion."[10] The nineteenth century seemed more than ever "a rather blurry, messy sort of a period, a rather sentimentalistic, mannerish sort of a period." *Ripostes,* the volume which Pound published at this moment of reassessment, when he had begun to plan a harder, more precise imagist poetry, reveals the changing sense of poetic values which accompanied—and probably preceded—his theorizing. The tone of the volume is defined by poems like the "Seafarer" translation, and "Δώρια," a love poem in the "Dorian" mood. A very simple poem, it offers little more than the designation of a mood which might be characterized as "restraint." The subject is psychological, a speaker presenting himself as stern and hard, excluding whatever gaiety or softness his character might have included. And the poem's form is equally restrained, avoiding the archaic words and the unusual syntax which Pound had employed in much of his earlier work. "Δώρια" does build on a rather simple, logical structure (take me in this way which is mine), but its force rests not in its argument, but in the pattern of concrete images which are offered as analogous to the speaker's mood—bleak wind, sunless cliffs, grey waters.

"Δώρια" is an obvious illustration of Pound's desire to replace the luxurious softness of a poetry imitative of the nineties with something harder—grey cliffs instead of shimmering jewels. But the poem's significant newness does not lie in its choice of subject—Pound never stopped writing about symbolically radiant light, and Pre-Raphaelite eyes—so much as in its greater economy of style. "A Girl," for example, treats the same subject as Pound's early poem, "The Tree"—the metamorphosis of a human being into a tree. Unlike the earlier poem, however, "A Girl" presents its strange transformation very simply and directly, assuming the girl's point of view and describing her experience in the present tense:

> The tree has entered my hands,
> The sap has ascended my arms,
> The tree has grown in my breast—
> Downward,
> The branches grow out of me, like arms.

By contrast, "The Tree" had placed the event in the past, and then proceeded to reflect about its meaning, describing the speaker's psychological experience and the knowledge which had come with it. "A Girl," on the other hand, offers only one such generalization ("And all this was folly to the world"), demanding instead that the reader infer any notions about the girl's feeling of wonder, or her new understanding from the description of what was literally happening. "The Tree" provides a particularly good contrast to Pound's later style because it is by no means one of his more elaborate or affected poems. And yet even so, the mannerisms of an older age abound: "wold," "T'was," "Nathless," "Unto the hearth of their heart's home." When Daphne becomes a laurel tree for the second time in Pound's verse, however, she does so with an economy and directness which minimizes our awareness of the poet, with his comments and conventions.

Aside from "The Seafarer," the most interesting poem in *Ripostes* is "Portrait d'une Femme." Though written in blank verse—a form which Pound was soon to condemn—the poem is in many ways as "modern" as Pound himself considered it.[11] The portrait is that of a woman who has spent twenty years at the center of London's artistic world, living a passive, even sterile life in which her only achievement has been to collect the thoughts of others. Like the Sargasso Sea, she seems a dead end, a collection of bits and pieces carried from a living world to rest with her in final stagnation. The poem's interest, however, lies in the interaction between this picture of a failed personality and the responses of the character who observes her. If most of the poem's "facts" seem to condemn her, the speaker's tone is far more ambiguous. In his explorations of the dramatic monologue, Pound had already learned to describe complex emotions, and his varying treatments of Bertran de Born had taught him that the same character can appear very different from different points of view. In "Portrait d'une Femme" he combines those insights to create a speaker whose mixture of scorn, fascination, and admiration makes it very difficult for us to know what the "true" nature of this woman is. Her reality is inseparable, in the poem, from the reality of the speaker's perceptions, and the result is an ambiguous picture of a life which seems rich, empty, learned, pointless, heroic, and, finally, puzzling. Most significantly, for his developing technique, Pound had accomplished this complex effect by means of a language which is far more flexible and free of artificiality than most of his earlier work, which can speak of "bright ships" and "this or that" in the same line. In a phrase like "you are a person of some interest," Pound avoids the need for comment and generalization by catching—in precisely chosen words—a tone which would praise but not without reservation; which offers emotion, but maintains a slightly defensive coolness. It was just this capacity to condense a complex of thought (what is she really like?) and emotion (how do I really feel about her?) into a single phrase or image, so avoiding abstract statement, that Pound was struggling to master in his imagist doctrine.

IV   *The Poetry of Imagism*

Ripostes was an uncertain volume, published when Pound's new doctrine had just begun to take clear shape in his mind.[12] It contains some evidence of his future direction, but there is also ambivalence, as, for example, in "N.Y.," where he speaks of the city in the language of pastoral verse at one point ("Thou art slender as a silver reed"), but elsewhere refers to traffic jams. The poem's attempt to counterpoint its two very different modes of perception is rather artificial, and Pound's uncertainty about how to move from old style to new is all too clear. Ezra Pound was not a tentative man, however, and by the spring of 1913 he was publishing poems, which were fully equal to his theories. Among them was "Tenzone," which now stands at the beginning of the "Lustra" section of *Personae*. Borrowing its title from an Italian, and ultimately Provençal, term for a verse dispute between poets, "Tenzone" announces Pound's new artistic direction in a tone which is closer to arrogance than uncertainty. Anticipating the public's failure to accept its new mode (or perhaps hoping to provoke such a response), Pound pictures himself as a centaur high up among crags which suggest the grey cliffs of "Δώρια." In its attitude toward the general public ("I beg you, my friendly critics,/Do not set about to procure me an audience"), "Tenzone" carries on a sense that art is for the initiated, not for the bourgeois masses—an attitude inherited from that very tradition of late nineteenth-century aestheticism which Pound was attempting to put behind him. But if the learned title, and the metaphor of the poet as disdainful centaur suggest an aesthete's pose, the poem's style has taken on a vigor and directness which already distinguish it from the languid symbolist atmosphere. Twenty years later he could renounce the elitist notion of art entirely: "For one thing, I don't care about 'minority culture.' I have never cared a damn about snobbisms or for writing *ultimately* for the few. Perhaps that is an exaggeration. Perhaps I was a worse young man than I think I was."[13] That was 1933, and he had the self-awareness to know that Pound young had indeed been something of an artistic snob. He knew the limits of that position early, however, and knew that his escape must be in fashioning a language that was hard, precise, and concrete.

In "Ité," another brief poem of that year, he addressed his own verse, charging it to "stand in the hard Sophoclean light." The sort of hard, demanding art he had in mind is clear enough, even if the tone and the images still celebrate the scornful artist betrayed by ignorant masses. Far more significant than these slight poems announcing the new program, however, were Pound's attempts to find his new language in practice. Among the first group of poems he published after *Ripostes* was one which quickly became the most famous, and purest, example of imagist verse, "In a Station of the Metro": "The apparition of these faces in the crowd;/Petals on a wet, black bough." Pound later described the evolution of this poem, which had its origin in an experience in the Paris metro. Encountering a series of beautiful faces as he stepped off a train, he had felt an emotion which seemed impossible to articulate. He struggled to find a means of expression, and came first to a vague intuition that, if he were a painter, he might be able to invent a new, "non-representative" style which "would speak only by arrangements in colour." And then he wrote a thirty-line poem, which he immediately destroyed, arriving at the extreme condensation of his final version only after a year's wait. As he describes the effect he was working toward, he makes it clear that he was primarily interested in the nature of perception itself: "In a poem of this sort one is trying to record the precise instant when a thing outward and objective transforms itself, or darts into a thing inward and subjective."[14] That is, he was interested in how we know the world beyond ourselves, how we see it, and how we sometimes respond with feeling. And more precisely, he wanted to discover how the immense complexity of that moment's perception might be caught in a poem. His answer was to trust the extreme simplicity of luminous detail to communicate experience, however complex, instantly and richly. "In a Station of the Metro" relies on just two images, both presented in a simple, direct way, plus the catalyst of one word which is not straightforward description: "apparition." Through the metaphoric suggestion of that word, Pound fuses the mundane image of "faces in the crowd," with an image possessing visual beauty and the rich connotations of countless poems about spring. And because "apparition" means what it does, he is able to convey the feeling of surprised discovery which such a vision in such a place must evoke.

One of the principles of Pound's practice at this time was that the rhetorical framework around metaphor should be stripped away, so that comparison, which is at the center of every metaphor, can be allowed to stand alone. For Pound, neither half of the comparison can be an abstraction; both must be concrete, precise images which, when juxtaposed, result in sudden illumination. Thus the blossoming tree and the anonymous urban faces leading to that startling discovery of ghostly beauty. But Pound was using the device in other poems too, as, for instance, in "April," where the image of olive boughs "stripped upon the ground" is followed by a closing line which suggests the death of people rather than leaves: "Pale carnage beneath bright mist." The scene is revealed to the speaker by "three spirits," and the poem's Latin epigraph ("the scattered limbs of the nymphs") suggests that some violent Dionysian rite has taken place. Both the human ritual, and the season of spring itself involve a natural cycle which leads from life to death to new life, endlessly. It is precisely that knowledge that the participants in Dionysian rite were being led to experience, and in Pound's poem the insight dawns with a complexity of emotion which goes far to justify his technique. Just as April seems nearly balanced between new growth and the deadness of winter, Pound's persona is pulled, emotionally, between the horror of "carnage" and the beauty and freshness of "bright mist." His revelation, witnessing dead leaves in April, is that his human life is also involved in the death which precedes birth.

As Pound explored the possibilities of his imagist theories, this capacity to evoke conflicting emotions, to communicate thought and feeling at the same moment, and with great economy, became one of his firmest achievements. He followed his own advice to "go in fear of abstractions," but not by taking the easy step of limiting his poems to small, mostly visual subjects. His imitators were soon doing that. Instead, he wrote about complex feeling, attempting to pare his language down to a spareness where image alone could accomplish what pages of discursive prose would only blur and falsify. In "The Spring," for example, he begins with a rather mythologized description of that season, with a procession of minor goddesses in a "sylvan place" where the vines are "clad in new brilliancies." But then he introduces new images, and a very slightly sketched plot:

> And wild desire
> Falls like black lightning.
> O bewildered heart,
> Though every branch have back what last year lost,
> She, who moved here amid the cyclamen,
> Moves only now a clinging tenuous ghost.

The experience is that of "Gentildonna," though the lady has been gone longer. The poem focuses on that moment when pain and loss are suddenly heightened by the intrusion of a contrary feeling—the joy of seeing new life in spring. T. S. Eliot used a generalization to say it ten years later: "April is the cruelest month." In Pound's poem, however, the shock of discovering pain and joy together is caught in the image of "black lightning," which communicates all its sudden, paradoxical feeling and which fuses the two contrary motifs of bright new growth, and bitter memory.

A similar effect occurs in "The Coming of War: Actaeon," another of Pound's poems about visionary experience. In this case the vision is of "hosts of an ancient people," who seem to return with the coming of war, bringing death. Again, there is very little in the way of comment or generalization, but the speaker's tone reveals a mixture of fear and admiration which is embodied in the imagery. A voice points out "Actaeon of the golden greaves!" and the gods move "over the cool face of that field," which is "full of faint light/but golden." Against the light and beauty of those images, however, Pound sets harsh, grey cliffs and a forbidding sea. The host of the gods is also described as "unstill, ever moving," associating them with that dark sea. The effect is to create a superficial impression of awe and wonder at the appearance of these gods, as they move across a rather beautiful field, perhaps at dawn. But that impression is immediately undercut by a sense of something else, dark and foreboding. In the sea and the granite and the restless moving, Pound communicates the intuition of a mind which knows, at some level, that these ghosts must be feared and avoided, at the same time that it regards their impressive approach with fascination.

Not all of Pound's poems during this period had been pared down to the ultimate simplicity of "In A Station of the Metro" or "Alba." Nor had he entirely abandoned generalization, which he was so quick to denounce in theory. But his work does show a continuous movement toward greater economy of statement, greater dependence on the suggestive power of images, and less use of the conventional mannerisms of nineteenth-century verse. Although poems like "April" and "Gentildonna" deal with perceptions, they offer only the slightest sense of character or situation, and the change in Pound's style is at least as apparent in those poems which attempt more. Throughout his explorations of dramatic lyric and persona, Pound had been fascinated by character—how it can be known, and how a poet can make his readers experience its particular qualities. With imagism, his interest continued, and along with his earlier techniques for recreating inner experience he added a new approach which was more "objective," viewing its characters from an external point of view. "The Garden" is an example of such a poem. It concerns a woman whose social position has schooled her in rules so narrow and repressive that she is trapped by her own fear and scorn. The first two lines of the poem establish her position precisely, as she walks in Kensington Gardens like "silk blown against a wall." Had the silk been a discarded newspaper, and the walk in Soho instead of the elegant Kensington, her nature would have seemed very different indeed. But Pound uses a cloth which is rich—and insubstantial—and in the next stanza he introduces "the filthy, sturdy, unkillable infants of the very poor," who frighten and disgust this delicate lady. But her character, and Pound's technique, are clearest in the last stanza:

> In her is the end of breeding.
> Her boredom is exquisite and excessive.
> She would like some one to speak to her,
> And is almost afraid that I
>   will commit that indiscretion.

Perhaps the greatest misunderstanding of imagism, by readers as well as by poets who quickly began to imitate it, was that it demanded visual images to the virtual exclusion of everything else. For Pound, however, imagism meant the achievement of a precise, economical verbal equation for emotion and idea. Though he often used visual images, the image was not a picture, but a structure of words. In his three initial rules, he asked for a rhythm free of artificial constraints, a ruthless pruning of all unnecessary words, and "direct treatment of the 'thing' whether subjective or objective." His doctrine was far more flexible and subtle than some of his imitators understood, and the concluding stanza of "The Garden" is a good illustration. While the first two lines do sound closer to generalization than we might expect, the rest of the stanza evokes the subtle complexity of the woman's social and emotional life by creating a complex of words which is fully as "luminous" as any detail of physical description: the ambiguity of "*almost* afraid," the suggestion of restriction in a syntax appropriate only to very formal usage ("that I will commit that indiscretion"), the connotations of "indiscretion" itself, a word used mostly to define the social proprieties of the upper classes. Just as her spontaneous humanity has been stifled by the demands of her class, so in the poem the pathetic temptation to human contact ("She would like some one to speak to her") is drowned out by the very words, and patterns of words, which have kept her fearful and isolated. Pound does not talk *about* her world—he shows it to us in the very kind of language which had shaped her view of its reality.

V   *The Great English Vortex*

In February, 1914, Pound published *Des Imagistes*, an anthology of imagist poetry which included among its contributors H. D., Richard Aldington, James Joyce, and Amy Lowell. Miss Lowell had come from Boston the previous year with a letter of introduction to Pound from Harriet Monroe, the editor of *Poetry*, and while they seemed at first to share an understanding of what needed to be done in American poetry, they soon found themselves at odds, primarily over Miss Lowell's determination to use her wealth for her own, and not Pound's, purposes. Their ill-feeling reached its peak in 1915 when she began publishing her own imagist anthologies with a large American publishing house which advertised her as "the foremost member of the Imagists," and simply listed Pound as one member of her group. Pound began to call the movement "Amygism," and refused to have anything more to do with it.

By 1914, however, Pound had already begun to think beyond imagism, which, at the hands of a host of minor poets, was soon to become a program for brief, pretty description. As his own earliest statements about imagism make clear, Pound understood the image to be *complex,* communicating intellectual as well as emotional meaning in a highly condensed way. Pound was interested in how the world can be known through images which fuse and focus the enormous complexities of external object and internal emotion. He said that an image "is more than an idea. It is a vortex or cluster of fused ideas and is endowed with energy."[15] At the level of perception and communication, "vortex" was a term which could name what Pound had begun to describe as early as his 1911 discussion of the luminous detail: a process by which the infinite variety of experience—meaningless in totality, and too easily falsified by generalization—might be known concretely.

There is a continuity in Pound's thought which critics have sometimes tended to obscure, with their descriptions of periods—preimagist, imagist, vorticist—which are not so distinct as they appear. The conceptual theories of Pound's vorticist period were less a departure from his previous thought than they were an elaboration and refinement. But vortex was not a word which Pound used exclusively to describe a process in the mind: "That is not 'the revival of classicism.' It is not a worship of corpses. It is an appreciation of the great Roman vortex, an understanding of, and an awakening to, the value of a capital, the value of centralization, in matters of knowledge and art, and of the interaction and stimulus of genius foregathered."[16] Pound saw another kind of vortex, a social one, in which the human and material resources of a nation could be gathered in one (or a few) centers, and like perceptions in the mind, focused. The result would be civilization, the equivalent, for society, of that awakening which Pound believed possible for individuals through the image. Nor was this notion purely theoretical for Pound. Just as the definition of vortex as a process of perception had derived from earlier ideas, so the vision of a *social* vortex capable of enriching and renewing our culture was an extension of Pound's hope for a new, American Renaissance. As he saw it, "a renaissance is a thing made—a thing made by conscious propaganda," and it was in this belief that his two conceptions of vortex could come together. All social change must have its beginning in the mind, and only through the artist's ability to purge away the extraneous data of history, forging images powerful enough to awaken individual men and women, could the collective awakening or renaissance take place.

The immediate outlet for such "propaganda" was a new magazine which Pound's friend Wyndham Lewis, the painter and novelist, was planning to publish in 1914. They called it *Blast:* "A Review of the Great English Vortex," and while only two issues were ever published, it succeeded in shocking most of England's literary establishment. Advertizing itself with the bold announcement, "End of Christian Era," *Blast* was filled with dogmatic pronouncements by Lewis, and poems by Pound which fully equaled the magazine's tone of harsh, satiric criticism. Most of the poems seem clearly minor, and some are surprisingly rhetorical. Pound did include some sharper, imagist verse, however, notably an epigram juxtaposing G. K. Chesterton and a new cake of soap (deleted from *Lustra* as possibly libelous), and a poem about shallow women attracted to the "false amber" in a shop window. Most memorable of the poems which depended on image rather than invective was "L'Art, 1910," where Pound set "green arsenic" beside "crushed strawberries," and then asked that we "feast our eyes." Pound may have been commenting on the post-Impressionist Exhibition, which opened in London in 1910, but whatever his specific target, the force of his image was clearly directed against the follies of an aesthetic movement so concerned with its own sensations that it could see no further than the surface color of a world badly in need of change.

If social satire was most prominent in Pound's poems from *Blast*, however, it was not his only concern at the time. Lewis was dogmatically a modernist, and Pound attempted at least one poem analagous to Lewis' painting, or the sculpture of Henri Gaudier-Brzeska and Jacob Epstein. "The Game of Chess," subtitled "Dogmatic Statement Concerning the Game of Chess: Theme for a Series of Pictures," follows the movement of modernist art away from representation and toward an emphasis on sheer form and color on the plane of the canvas itself. But Pound also continued to write poems which were neither harshly satiric nor consciously "modernist." "The Gypsy" was one such poem, carrying on his exploration of how the uniqueness of character and place and moment might be communicated. Drawing on his experience of walking the roads of Provence, it simply records his meeting with a gypsy who had become separated from his fellows. Although there is no attempt at psychological depth, the particularity of the experience is caught by a few simple, precise details: wind and rain, "the wet road near Clermont," a long walk through gray towns already behind him, and, most of all, the "apes or bears" about which the gypsy inquires.

In poems like "The Gypsy," Pound was refining one of his earliest poetic interests, recording the texture of experience in a world defined by details which were becoming less mystical, and more realistic. But he was also learning, in other poems, to extend the range of his context and his tone to include the social protest of *Blast,* and even to contemplate the more radical innovations of the plastic arts, with their possible consequences for poetry. Most of all, however, he had learned, by 1915, to consolidate the technical achievements of imagism, and to begin to use them as part of a more inclusive, flexible, socially aware program for poetry.

CHAPTER 4

Discovering China

I *Imagism and Chinese Verse*

WHEN Pound described the year-long process by which he composed "In a Station of the Metro," he referred to the completed poem as "a hokku-like sentence." And for many readers of imagist verse, the resemblance to the precise economy of haiku and other Eastern forms is immediate and inevitable. Pound was fully conscious of the analogy, and among the imagist poems which he was writing in 1913 were four adaptations from the Chinese. Knowing very little about either the language or the poetic conventions of China, he simply worked with English translations which he found in H. A. Giles' *A History of Chinese Literature* (1901). Whatever his value as literary historian, Giles, as poet, was trapped by the verbal clichés of Victorian sentiment:

> And yet I fear, ah me! that autumn chills,
> Cooling the dying summer's torrid rage,
> Will see thee laid neglected on the shelf,
> All thought of bygone days, like them bygone.[1]

These words were addressed to her silk fan by a former mistress of the emperor, who had tired of her, and when Pound came to make a new poem out of them, he revealed the fundamental thrust of his imagist program. The ten lines of Giles' version became just three for Pound, who stripped away all the rhetorical sentiment ("ah me!"), and the worn-out poetic diction ("bygone days," "dying summer's torrid rage"), fashioning instead a poem which condenses the dramatic situation and its emotion into the single image of a white silk fan which has "also" been laid aside. "Fan-Piece, For Her Imperial Lord" achieves its effect by first purging away all distracting, rhetorical conventions, so that the reader's attention is focused clearly on the image of the fan, and then it charges that image with emotional significance in the last line, through subtle implication. The fan has been laid aside, and by simply inserting his "also" Pound evokes a drama involving betrayal and rejection, though, as he wrote to Williams in 1908, the details do not interest him. What does, is the emotional moment, the sense of sadness and despair which had already been prepared by the image of frost on the grass blade: visually beautiful, but portending death.

In "Ts'ai Chi'h," Pound used a similar technique to create a typically imagist fragment which is even slighter in its content: rose leaves fall into a fountain, and "their ochre clings to the stone." There is no suggestion of plot at all, only the vague sense of sadness at life passing away, evoked by a traditional image of flowers disintegrating to dust and stain against the permanence of stone. A slightly fuller treatment of a similar theme is "Liu Ch'e," taken, like "Fan-Piece" and "After Ch'u Yuan," from Giles. There is some suggestion of plot, in the setting which is deserted now but which once knew life, and in the speaker's apparent reference to the death of his beloved: "The rustling of the silk is discontinued." Pound builds his image (which does not simply mean "picture") by such effects as the deft juxtaposition of romantic diction ("rustling of the silk") with a bureaucratic word ("discontinued") which ends the line like a disappointed promise. Drifting dust and the piles of dead leaves help to focus the impression that something has ended, but the poem's effect really depends on the last line, where a leaf which is fallen, wet, clearly bound for death, nevertheless "clings" to the threshold. The leaf embodies a tenacious attachment to life in the face of death which is like the speaker's affection for his dead lover— hopelessly persisting. His feeling is the poem's subject, and Pound communicates it without direct statement or elaborate "plot." His practice in these first attempts to approximate Chinese verse—which are not so much translations as rewritings of inferior English poems—was primarily a part of his exploration of the imagist principles which he had only recently laid down. Even under the nineteenth-century surface of Giles' versions, he saw a poetry which avoided rhetoric, which valued economy and precision, and which knew how to communicate human emotion through the suggestive power of its images — particularly those drawn from nature. Chinese poetry, however, was about to become far more important for Pound than it had been as an interesting, minor analogy to imagist theory.

II   *Ernest Fenollosa*

During the 1870s an American named Ernest Fenollosa had gone to Japan to become an instructor in rhetoric at the Imperial University. Fascinated by Chinese and Japanese art, he had worked to conserve their traditions as a collector, a student of language and literature, and eventually as imperial commissioner of art. He died in 1908, and in 1913 his widow was introduced to Ezra Pound in London. Having read some of his poetry, she felt that she had finally found someone to whom she might entrust her husband's papers — sixteen notebooks filled with transcriptions, literal translations, and glosses of Chinese and Japanese poetry and Noh dramas, plus her husband's essay on "The Chinese Written Character As A Medium for Poetry." Fenollosa had considered his material more significant as literature than as philology, and in choosing to make Pound literary executor, Mrs. Fenollosa had guessed — brilliantly — that he would be able to release the poetry in her scholar husband's very unpoetic jottings.

During that winter, of 1913-1914, Pound was living in the country with W. B. Yeats, acting as secretary (and unofficial instructor in modernism) to the older poet. Both men were fascinated by the Noh drama, and Pound's first undertaking was to edit a translation, by Fenollosa, of *Nishikigi*, which he published in *Poetry* early in 1914. For the poet who was just then attempting to rethink all his assumptions about what poetry ought to be, however, Fenollosa's essay on "The Chinese Written Character As A Medium for Poetry" was most interesting. And while Pound had great difficulty — for years — in finding a publisher for the essay, it eventually assumed the central place in twentieth-century poetic theory which Pound began to claim for it almost at once. Fenollosa had written the essay as a kind of refutation of the more unimaginative scholars of Oriental language, emphasizing the poetic qualities of Chinese verse, which seemed to him both remarkable, and very poorly understood. The starting point for his argument was the notion that the Chinese ideograph is not primarily phonetic, that it preserves the concrete, pictorial representation which had been its origin. He describes the character for "man" as consisting of two legs, and that for "sees" as a picture of an eye, with two legs running beneath it. Though more recent scholarship has demonstrated that Chinese writing is indeed phonetic, Fenollosa's mistaken premise could not have been more attractive to Pound, who had already begun to warn other poets to "go in fear of abstractions." And Fenollosa's assumptions about the Chinese language were really not as important for Pound's endeavor as were his assumptions about poetry. Above all, Fenollosa was clear and vigorous in his denunciation of abstraction as entirely destructive of poetic values. Against the concrete quality of Chinese written words, he saw the tendency toward abstraction as basic to a European culture which had inherited "the tyranny of medieval logic." Comparing thought, under this system of logic, to a brickyard, he describes it as "baked into hard little units or concepts," which can then be stuck together to form sentences through the mortar of "is" and "is not." This process of abstraction, "building pyramids of attenuated concept until we reach the apex 'being,'" distorts our perceptions of the world, trapping our thought in rigid categories, and doing most violence to those *things* which lie, "stunned, as it were," at the bottom of the pyramid.

Against that tradition of abstracting logic and language, Fenollosa sets a poetry which communicates all the rich concreteness of the world, by drawing on the resources of an ideographic writing which, for example, represents "east" by a picture of the sun tangled in the branches of a tree. Such a poetry respects the surface reality of its world, while avoiding that logic which organizes our perceptions by forcing them into separate, narrowly defined categories. This does not mean, however, that Fenollosa advocates a poetry concerned solely with "objective" description: "Such actions are *seen*, but Chinese would be a poor language, and Chinese poetry but a narrow art, could they not go on to represent also what is unseen. The best poetry deals not only with natural images but with lofty thoughts, spiritual suggestions and obscure relations."[2] From the time of his earliest experiments in symbolist evocation, Pound had been interested in poetry which could suggest a reality beyond the visible, and he preserved that interest, even after his imagist doctrines had led him to denounce the outworn softness of his earlier models and embrace a poetry of verbal economy and concrete image. His image was a luminous point, chosen from a field of countless real things, and capable of leading to that flash of sudden understanding, emotional as well as intellectual, which Pound valued above all else. In Fenollosa's essay, he found the description of a virtually unknown poetic system—though the product of one of the world's greatest civilizations—which was praised for its capacity to communicate in precisely that way.

For both Fenollosa and Pound, the means by which poetry accomplishes its complex illumination is metaphor, and a metaphor condensed into language which is simple and precise, but powerfully evocative: "Poetic thought works by suggestion, crowding maximum meaning into the single phrase pregnant, charged, and luminous from within."[3] This statement by Fenollosa should be set beside Pound's imagist insistence on using "absolutely no word that does not contribute to the presentation," and his faith in the luminous detail to carry as much complex, significant meaning as pages of generalizing prose. For Fenollosa, the word in all poetry is "like a sun, with its corona and chromosphere; words crowd upon words, and enwrap each other in their luminous envelopes until sentences become clear, continuous light-bands." Even the metaphor of light reinforces a conception of poetic revelation which Pound drew first from radiant Pre-Raphaelite ladies, and later from the symbolism of medieval poetry, and which he carried as far as the latest *Cantos*.

Just as important as the support Fenollosa's essay gave to Pound's new poetic theories, was its larger philosophical arguments. Fenollosa saw concrete metaphor as capable of communicating such rich and valid insight into the world because he believed it to be firmly rooted in the very reality it would describe. Rejecting the Western tendency to break the world up into countless separated parts in our minds (thoughts as bricks), he saw instead a universe in which "all processes in nature are interrelated." If all language began in metaphor, as he believed, that process was nevertheless not arbitrary or merely subjective, because it grew very directly out of the patterns of nature itself:

Relations are more real and more important than the things which they relate. The forces which produce the branch-angles of an oak lay potent in the acorn. Similar lines of resistance, half-curbing the out-pressing vitalities, govern the branching of rivers and of nations. Thus a nerve, a wire, a roadway, and a clearing-house are only varying channels which communication forces for itself. This is more than analogy, it is identity of structure. Nature furnishes her own clues. Had the world not been full of homologies, sympathies, and identities, thought would have been starved and language chained to the obvious. There would have been no bridge whereby to cross from the minor truth of the seen to the major truth of the unseen.[4]

As Pound moved through the period of imagist revaluation, and toward the major work of his *Cantos*, this vision of a world in complex, continuous interdependence became more and more central to his thought. He learned to see the fascination of pattern itself, and he used the insight to bring together his wide range of interests: poetic craft; social oppression; the history of Europe, China, and America; a natural world of great beauty and, perhaps, spiritual significance. If the world is one, if everything is in patterned relation to everything else, then all these apparently separate concerns are related too. The culture of the present flows out of the past, just as language flows out of nature, and in metaphor the repeating patterns of our human society, our inner lives, and the natural world around us cross and, perhaps, become visible. Pound had already begun to formulate a philosophy based on the perception of nature as wholly alive and wholly inclusive, with language as the key to its patterns, but in Fenollosa's essay he found the words he needed: "metaphor, the revealer of nature, is the very substance of poetry. The known interprets the obscure, the universe is alive with myth."

III Cathay: *Imagism and Translation*

Pound's first poetic use of the Fenollosa material was in *Cathay*, a volume of just fifteen poems, published in 1915. Aside from his translation of "The Seafarer," which was reprinted in this collection, the poems were all based on Fenollosa's notes— literal, word-for-word glosses under transcriptions of the original Chinese characters, followed by a more grammatical English version and perhaps a commentary.[5] As material for poetry, the glosses were bare bones indeed, and the English versions were

little better. Fenollosa was not always a reliable guide, and
traditional academic scholars were delighted to point out
mistakes which were sometimes Fenollosa's and sometimes
Pound's—such as his taking two separate poems in the notebook
to be a single poem, and merging them into what became "The
River Song." More recent scholars, however, have begun to
demonstrate that Pound's "mistakes" were sometimes brilliantly
intuitive of qualities in the Chinese originals which Fenollosa had
obscured completely.[6] And for many of Pound's critics, the
merits of *Cathay* as translation were less important than its more
generally recognized value as significant new English poetry.
What Pound accomplished in *Cathay* was the application of
imagist principles of composition to poems which had previously
been translated only into the overelaborate and sometimes
precious diction of late nineteenth-century verse. He created a
style whose lucid simplicity seemed to parallel the precise use of
line and space in a Japanese watercolor, and the effect was so
immediately convincing that T. S. Eliot, in 1928, called him "the
inventor of Chinese poetry for our time."[7] In a brief poem like
"The Beautiful Toilet," for instance, Pound places a few simple
images in juxtaposition, letting their suggestive power define the
mood of a young woman who has been left alone by her drunken
husband:

> Blue, blue is the grass about the river
> And the willows have overfilled the close garden.
> And within, the mistress, in the midmost of her youth,
> White, white of face, hesitates, passing the door.
> Slender, she puts forth a slender hand.

Some of the poem's qualities do represent conventions of
Chinese verse, such as the repetition of words—though Pound
varies the technique from line to line to avoid the monotony that
Western readers might feel. But the poem achieves its effect
primarily through images of nature which, if traditional to
Chinese verse, also conform perfectly to imagist doctrine. The
willows have "overfilled" a garden which is "close" (enclosed,
but inevitably carrying the more common meaning as well),
while the woman, who is "within" and also in the "midmost" of
her youth, reaches out through the door in a simple, hesitant
gesture which focuses all the oppressive sense of enclosure built

up by the previous lines. And then Pound introduces the "facts" of her situation—that she had been a "courtezan," and that her husband is a "sot." Having known the freedom and excitement of a life among people, perhaps at court, the young woman's aura of innocent, wasting youth, created in the first stanza, is complicated by irony in the second. With only the simplest details of plot, Pound charges the poem's images (grass, trees, garden) and its single action (the slender hand reaching out) with a rich complexity of emotion which involves (at least) loneliness, regret, yearning, perhaps bitterness, a feeling of being trapped, and the necessity to live in memory many years too soon.

Though all the poems in *Cathay* reflect Pound's imagist values to some extent, one of the purest examples is "The Jewel Stairs' Grievance." The poem is very brief, consisting of just four lines which describe jeweled steps white with dew, dew soaking the gauze stockings of the woman who speaks, and then her action of opening a curtain and watching the moon. Pound added a note which tells us a great deal about how he thought a poem should be read, as well as what he valued in poetry at the time:

Jewel stairs, therefore a palace. Grievance, therefore there is something to complain of. Gauze stockings, therefore a court lady, not a servant who complains. Clear autumn, therefore he has no excuse on account of weather. Also she has come early, for the dew has not merely whitened the stairs, but has soaked her stockings. The poem is especially prized because she utters no direct reproach.

In commenting on the poem so explicitly, Pound offers a clear explanation of how much information he expects his images to bear. Character and setting, for instance, are defined by just two details: jeweled stairs and gauze stockings. Like "The Beautiful Toilet," this poem builds its story—of a woman whose lover has failed to appear at their rendezvous—out of a series of small details which then come to focus in an action which, by itself, would seem meaningless: opening a curtain, watching the moon. Properly prepared, however, that action implies all the feelings of anger and disappointment which "grievance" would lead us to expect. In these two poems, Pound was working toward the achievement, in practice, of what his imagist theories had described: the creation of images which convey meanings of great complexity and power to move, in far less space than would have been possible in any of the old, abstracting forms of discourse.

Throughout *Cathay*, Pound applied his imagist techniques, with a variety of consequences. In addition to the use of "luminous details" to communicate the complex emotions of particular situations, he avoided any hint of elaborate, unnecessary diction. Sometimes his language was very informal, even conversational. But even where his tone was less colloquial, he followed the imagist dictum that poets must use "no word that does not contribute to the presentation." Thus "clear autumn" (in "Jewel Stairs' Grievance") not only tells us about the weather, but also carries its traditional associations to a human relationship which, like the year, is dying. The same careful choice of words is true of "Separation on the River Kiang," a poem about friends parting:

> Ko-jin goes west from Kō-kaku-ro,
>   The smoke-flowers are blurred over the river.
> His lone sail blots the far sky.
> And now I see only the river,
>   The long Kiang, reaching heaven.

Puffs of smoke or mist which had looked like flowers become "blurred," while the sail actually growing smaller as the boat recedes, appears so large to the speaker that it "blots" the sky. Pound reveals emotion by showing us emotion's power to distort perceptions. And in choosing precisely the words he does, he also communicates a sense that something has been destroyed by this parting, that a transitory beauty has been shown to be insubstantial ("smoke-flowers"), blurring and finally disappearing in the emptiness of the last line. Any one of the poems in *Cathay* could offer such examples of diction and image chosen precisely, and then manipulated to convey the greatest amount of insight—generally into some emotionally charged human situation—with the least amount of supporting explanation. Imagism had already ceased to be a public program for Pound, but its method had become a permanent part of his craft.

IV   *A Poetry of Departures*

Hugh Kenner has described *Cathay* as Pound's poetic response to World War I: "Its exiled bowmen, deserted women, levelled dynasties, departures for far places, lonely frontier guardsmen and glories remembered from afar, cherished memories, were selected from the diverse wealth in the notebooks by a sensibility responsive to torn Belgium and disrupted London."[8] Many of Pound's friends had gone to the war—men like T. E. Hulme, Ford Maddox Hueffer, and the sculptor, Henri Gaudier-Bzreska—and some, Gaudier and Hulme among them, would die there. The elegiac tone is pervasive in *Cathay*, in poem after poem about exile and separation, and sometimes literally about the sorrows of war. "Song of the Bowmen of Shu" and "South-Folk in Cold Country" both deal with the emotions of warriors far from home, as does "Lament of the Frontier Guard," which pictures the "desolate fields" of a distant outpost. "Lament" builds its mood of lonely despair through a series of images suggesting death and emptiness: sand blowing in the wind, grass turning yellow, bones, frost, ruined castles, empty sky. Pound sets the poem in a time of waiting, the speaker looking out on a desolate, alien landscape, questioning the men who have made this war, and anticipating his own inevitable death. His tone suggests a mixture of helpless anger, loneliness, and despair.

In "Song of the Bowmen of Shu" Pound offers a similar view, once again adopting the persona of a weary soldier on some distant frontier. He suggests the slow passage of time, and the increasing privation of the bowmen's lives by an image which seems to be repeating, but which is really undergoing a subtle metamorphosis: "Here we are, picking the first fern-shoots," and then, four lines later, "We grub the soft fern-shoots," and finally "We grub the old fern-stalks." Picking becomes grubbing, soft drops out, to be replaced by old, and shoots become stalks: as the season grows, the soldiers' plight grows too, and what had been a pleasant search for fiddleheads becomes a desperate need to eat anything, even the almost inedible stalks of the mature fern. Like "Lament," the poem is filled with questioning, about when the warriors will go home, who has caused the war, and whether anyone knows or cares about their fate. The language is simple and direct, often relying on images which are charged with human significance through their juxtaposition with statements just explicit enough to establish the situation: the soldiers set out while willows are "drooping with spring," but when they return there is snow on the ground. There is a sense of inevitability about the poem, and a weary foreboding. And most of all, there is the feeling of being alone, abandoned: "who will know of our sorrow?"

The poems of *Cathay* were certainly responding to the dislocations of a war which had already drawn away the best of the young British artists, shattering the great cultural vortex which Pound had hoped to initiate in London. But the war was not Pound's only concern at the time, and *Cathay* stands at a crucial point in his developing sense of what his task as an artist would be. Pound began his career as a poet surrounded by the aura of symbolist and decadent verse. He wrote in their language—sensuous, romantic, distanced by strange old words— and he wrote about the mysterious ladies, and the rare moments of perception and intense emotion which he had found in their verse. It was largely a cult of Beauty, refining its aesthetic responses in a private world of poetry, and shutting out the detested bourgeoisie, with their materialism, their sentimentality, and their moralizing rhetoric. Pound had gone on to study the literature of medieval Provence, and there he had found a rich field for his play with the beauties of archaic, distant things. By 1912, that part of his life was over. When Ford Maddox Hueffer rolled on the floor in derision at the hopelessly old-fashioned diction of *Canzoni*, Pound knew that he had been indulging himself, following the conventions of an outworn age when he should have been looking to the shape of his own century. He set out to purge his style of all the affectation of archaic words and nineteenth-century mannerism, and as his friendship with artists like Gaudier-Brzeska and Wyndham Lewis grew, he began to think about what a modernist style in poetry might be like. Nor did his disenchantment with the nineteenth-century roots of his art stem entirely from the need to find a newer style. Pound had always been a social reformer in some part of himself, and as the impulse grew to alter the course of what seemed to be a culture increasingly destructive of human values, he saw, and rejected, the symbolist tendency to cultivate private sensation at the expense of a responsibility to the public good.

Imagism and vorticism were the first two names for Pound's endeavor to make a new poetry for the present and the future. But in 1915 there was, as yet, no *Waste Land*, no *Ulysses*, and no *Cantos*. Unlike the graphic arts, the modernist period in literature was only beginning, and against the uncertainties of the future, Pound had to weigh a tradition from the past which he could no longer accept, even though it had moved him deeply and always would. It was a time for separation from some of his oldest commitments, and because his vision of what the new age demanded set him more violently than ever against the prevailing values of British and American culture, he felt himself all the more an exile. *Cathay* is a book about just such feelings:

> Blue mountains to the north of the walls,
> White river winding about them;
> Here we must make separation
> And go out through a thousand miles of dead grass.

These lines are from "Taking Leave of a Friend," one of the "Four Poems of Departure." The poem's tone is elegiac, projecting its emotion primarily through the images of dead grass and, in the next stanza, sunset ("Sunset like the parting of old acquaintances"). But these deathlike images, meaningful on the emotional level, are accompanied by a rather decisive sense that a point has been reached ("Here we must make separation") at which a turning toward new directions must be accepted. The speaker seems to know that a changed future is inevitable, even as he feels the pain of breaking old attachments.

Pound's fullest treatment of the emotions of loss and separation is in "Exile's Letter," a translation of a poem by Li Po, China's greatest poet. Adopting the persona form, Pound presents Li Po as tradition has preserved him—a man concerned chiefly with music and courtesans and drink. The poem is set in a time of exile for the speaker, who is far from all he has loved, but it takes the form of a letter to his old friend, and consists primarily of a recollection of past happiness, which is made all the more poignant by an insistent past tense, reminding us of his present condition. Donald Davie describes him as "a drunkard, an idler, disreputable, undependable, without self-respect,"[9] but while that may be history's judgment of Li Po, it is not quite Pound's. His character does indeed remain drunk "for month on month," delighting most in memories of "a jewelled mouth-organ" and courtesans with eyebrows painted green, "dancing in transparent brocade." But the poem's strongest impression is not of his irresponsibility, but rather of his sensitivity. Unrecognized by the court, and so failing to achieve one of the civil service positions reserved for literary men, the poet is forced to live and write in the obscurity of exile. And there, dreaming of the past, his affirmation that there is "no end of things in the heart" is the same one that Pound, in his own exile in an American army prison camp thirty years later, recorded in the *Pisan Cantos:* "What thou lovest well remains, / the rest is dross."

The elegiac mood moves through a variety of poetic occasions in *Cathay.* In "Poem By the Bridge At Ten-Shin," for example, the speaker laments the fact that "to-day's men are not the men of the old days," and he dreams about dead heroes who have been swept away like peach blossoms "on the gone waters." "The River-Merchant's Wife: A Letter," on the other hand, creates a persona whose dilemma is more particular. The young wife of the poem has been left alone by her husband, whose trade carries him far away, and she recalls their first meeting as children, their marriage when she was only fourteen, and then her slowly growing love. Having adopted the wife's point of view, Pound is able to define her feelings by having her perceive a series of images onto which she projects her own emotions: monkeys making what seems to her a "sorrowful noise," mosses accumulating by the gate, falling leaves. The persona who emerges in the poem exhibits a kind of psychological opening-out, growing from the hermetic bashfulness of childhood into a capacity for self-awareness and self-expression which is direct and moving, though always balanced by a tone of dignified formality. Once again, however, the predominant effect of the poem is to convey a mood of loss and separation.

Whatever the particular occasion, it is that mood which dominates *Cathay.* Most often, the dramatic situation of the poem involves a character suffering the loneliness of isolation or exile, like the speaker in "To-Em-Mei's (t' ao ch' ien) 'The Unmoving Cloud,' "[10] who stays in his room alone, estranged from friends, and wistfully pats his new cask of wine. No more interested in the details of plot than he was in 1908, when he dismissed it as merely "the prose part" of the drama, Pound emphasizes his character's emotion, at a moment when he is intensely aware of his own plight. The practice of focusing his poems on such moments of emotionally significant experience was habitual with Pound, though in *Cathay* the range of feeling tends to be smaller, and more of a piece. "The Unmoving Cloud" employs images of gathering clouds, rain, an empty road, and still another (pre-*Waste Land*) ironic spring to state its desolate mood. Of the fourteen poems which Pound chose to recast out of the many more available in Fenollosa's notes, this tone of sorrow is by far the most noticeable. Combined with the certainty that something had ended, and with a nostalgia for those lost times, the elegiac note of *Cathay* served, in 1915, to mark a final departure from the nineteenth century, which Pound shared with all of Europe, as he turned to the tasks of a new age, and to the uncertainty of a future clouded by war.

V   *The Search for Social Conscience*

Even during the height of his fascination with the aesthetic movements of the nineties, Pound had cared about social justice, about the state of culture in England as well as back home in the America he had left. What he saw depressed him, but he was a stubborn optimist, and his faith in the possibility for change drove him to imagine a different world. A student of the early Renaissance in Italy, he also had a tendency to read history with an eye for repeating patterns, for parallels between distant ages. Thus in *Cathay*, he set "The Seafarer," recording the painful isolation which one man had known in England in Anglo-Saxon times against a series of ancient Chinese poems dealing with the same human experience. And studying the Renaissance, he saw the vitalizing effect which new access to the languages and literatures of the classical world had had. Pound saw no reason why America in the twentieth century should not undergo as great a reawakening, and in 1914 he wrote an essay, called "The Renaissance," in which he considered how it might be brought to pass: "The last century rediscovered the middle ages. It is possible that this century may find a new Greece in China."[11] As he saw it, the state would have to begin to value art and artists, and it would have to nurture the vortex (imaginatively, an atmosphere; literally, a great city) which alone could draw alien traditions together to create a new age of cultural vitality: "If you so endow sculptors and writers you will begin for America an age of awakening which will over-shadow the quattrocento; because our opportunity is greater than Leonardo's: we have more aliment, we have not one classic tradition to revivify, we have China and Egypt, and the unknown lands lying upon the roof of the world—Khotan, Kara-shar and Kan-su."[12] If "Kara-shar and Kan-su" were a bit of rhetorical exuberance on Pound's part, China was not. The example of Chinese culture seemed steadily more impressive to him over the years, Confucian thought in particular, and even in this first full-scale venture into Oriental art, some of his later interests are already evident. Although *Cathay* seems to be entirely a study of sensibility, a careful portrait of men and women experiencing a narrow range of feeling, its background does imply larger, social concerns.

In "Song of the Bowmen of Shu," for example, the suffering of the men is a result of war, and while the speaker accepts its necessity, and sees the barbarian enemy as aggressor, there is nevertheless some awareness that the bowmen's plight is harsher than that of the generals. "Lament of the Frontier Guard" paints an even bleaker picture of the human desolation wrought by the warring of "barbarous kings." If *Cathay* does speak indirectly to the emotions of World War I, it also speaks about social consequences which Pound was to describe most bitterly in *Hugh Selwyn Mauberley.* Justified or not, war, to the people, means only "sorrow, sorrow like rain,/Sorrow to go, and sorrow, sorrow returning." In "South-Folk in Cold Country" the speaker, another warrior in a desolate land, far from home, says that "Hard fight gets no reward./Loyalty is hard to explain." Focusing so exclusively on the suffering and the pointlessness of war, Pound implicitly identifies with the people, who die, against the generals who send them to die. Pound's battlefields are empty and desolate, his heroes merely doomed survivors.

Cathay stands at a critical point in the development of Pound's art and thought. Looking back with sadness to an outworn age, it was also a volume which looked ahead to a world exhausted and demoralized by war. *Cathay* anticipated a mood which everyone knew by 1922, when Eliot named it in *The Waste Land.* But Pound, in 1915, was already looking for alternatives to the cheapness, the waste, the social injustice he saw all around him, and in Fenollosa's China he found a precedent for his hope, as well as an image to fit the mood of a sorrowful Europe. The China of *Cathay* contained war, private injustice, and some of the qualities of a corrupt, superficial society, but it also preserved a place for art, with its capacity to make the values, the emotions, and the sins of an age visible. In Pound's reading of the Italian Renaissance, the artist held a central place in the moral and aesthetic renewal of his society, and as Pound looked through the glass of China to America's own awakening, he saw a similar pattern. He had found his new Greece, and soon, in Confucius, he would find his Aristotle.

CHAPTER 5

Poet and Society

I Satiric verse

THE poems of *Cathay* are characterized almost uniformly by an elegant, precise surface and by a tone which is contemplative and elegiac. In 1915, they were right, emotionally, for a poet who was forsaking a part of his old life to enter an age desperately in need of new forms. His society, through the shock of war, was experiencing its own belated transition to the new century, and while Pound shared its crisis in many ways, he also felt himself more isolated than ever, more compelled to speak against the shallow materialism and the disdain for artistic values which he saw all around him. *Cathay* marked a significant point in Pound's developing sense of craft and in his search for the materials of his future poetic endeavor, but it was by no means all he was writing at the time. In 1914 and 1915 he was also involved in vorticism with Wyndham Lewis, publishing poems of harsh social criticism in *Blast,* and in a good many other periodicals. There was a kind of split in his work for a time, the sensitive, lyrical treatment of emotion so evident in his Chinese translations finding no place in the poems dedicated to a witty, and sometimes savage criticism of society's follies.

As a poet who had begun to learn how language might be shaped by experimenting with the persona form, Pound knew that style is not so much the simple, direct expression of an author's character as it is a method to be chosen consciously, from among many possibilities, and that it should be varied with varying artistic purposes. Of the several styles which Pound began to explore about 1913, one issued in poems which were short, aggressive in tone, and direct and colloquial in diction.

Rhetorical, and given to exaggerated poses, they seem less significant than the imagist experiments which led to clearly major changes in the techniques of twentieth-century verse, nor do they offer the sort of lyrical beauty which made *Cathay* more immediately appealing than most of Pound's volumes.[1] But Pound was experimenting with ideas as well as technique, and the style of these poems is largely a reflection of his attempt to articulate a slowly building anger whose object was society's injustice and stupidity. The poems clarified his social stance in ways which were an indispensable preparation for all his future work. Among the issues they treated, one of the most important was the question of how the artist ought to relate to his own society. The sort of response of the average, popular critic to Pound's modern verse, which he imagines in "Salutation the Second," is central to his analysis:

> "Is this," they say, "the nonsense
> > that we expect of poets?"
> "Where is the Picturesque?"
> > "Where is the vertigo of emotion?"
> "No! his first work was the best."
> > "Poor Dear! he has lost his illusions."

As Pound saw it, the critical expectations of his day excluded any poetry that was truly serious, considering verse instead to be "nonsense," an entertaining, but meaningless fiction. The critics were patronizing, explaining away any art which seemed overly serious by recourse to the sort of easy put-down of the last line. To say that an artist has "lost his illusions," however, reveals a romantic, even sentimental view of the poet passing from innocence, to suffering, to cynicism which is fundamental to the critical assumptions which Pound had set out to challenge. For his imagined critic, poetry could offer a thrill of emotion ("vertigo" suggests the easy manipulation of feeling of a roller coaster), and it could frame a "picturesque" charm which was in no way disturbing or threatening. What it could not do is depart from the critic's narrow, conventional expectations regarding form, or, more serious, question the values and customs of its present-day audience.

In rejecting the timid, outdated precepts of a criticism that spoke for the mass of readers, Pound was also rejecting his own

early poetry. In poems like "Epilogue" he made very clear his
estimation of those poems which had once "created considerable
stir in Chicago," but which he now regarded as "stale and worn
out." Representing "a very depleted fashion" in his eyes, that
poetry which he had made out of the leftover aura of the nineties
was wrong in every way but one, and that one the principle
which he never doubted: "Only emotion remains." However
transient the connections of style might be, the feelings they
record are real beyond any shift of taste. Granted the enduring
validity of experience, however, poetic conventions which have
come to seem false may illuminate social and psychological
attitudes which are equally false. "The Lake Isle," for example,
is a parody of W. B. Yeats' "The Lake Isle of Innisfree," a poem
of 1890 about a man's yearning, in the city, for the peace of a
solitary retreat in the country. Indulging itself in the suggestive
beauty of images which illustrate the symbolist doctrine of
"precise vagueness," Yeats' poem was an evasion of the artist's
responsibility to confront the reality of his own society—as Yeats
himself came reluctantly to know. Pound's satire reduced the
conventional visionary yearning of the nineties to the essentially
trivial and negative escapism that it was:

> O God, O Venus, O Mercury, patron of thieves,
> Lend me a little tobacco-shop,
>   or install me in any profession
> Save this damn'd profession of writing,
>   where one needs one's brains all the time.

It had been Yeats and his world of Celtic twilight who among all
living poets had served as Pound's first model, but Pound had
grown away from that mode (and hoped to take Yeats with him),
and his defection was not only a matter of changing fashion but a
realization that the evils of society must be addressed boldly, not
masked by a defensively beautiful, archaic diction.

Rejecting the selfishness of the commercial artist who *uses*
society, as well as that of the aesthete, who ignores it, Pound
would serve the genuine needs of the people by confronting
their problems in poetry which offered no artistic compromise,
and which defined those needs on its own terms. In this respect,
Pound was firmly in the tradition of American reformers, and for
all his cosmopolitanism, that background is evident in his way of

perceiving contemporary society. "Society," for example, a little epigram about a young girl willing to sell herself to an old man for the sake of money and "family position" strikes to the heart of Pound's vision of social wrong. Above all else he detested any ethic which places money ahead of the dignity of human worth. Writing in *Patria Mia*, he had said that " 'The first duty of a nation is to conserve its human resources.' I believe that this sentence contains the future greatness of America. I believe that because of this perception we shall supersede any nation that attempts to conserve first its material resources."[2] It was this vision of a free and just society, or as he put it elsewhere, a new American Renaissance, that lay behind Pound's denunciation of the sort of debasing social ethic which "Society" pictures.

That social bondage, sexuality, and money are related in Pound's epigram was no accident. He understood their interrelationship very clearly, and in "Commission" he made the most unequivocal statement of his insight into "unconscious oppression," that subtle tyranny of countless suburbs over "the bought wife." Like William Blake's "mind forg'd manacles," the bondage which Pound saw is mostly unconscious, the result of social constraints so deep as to be invisible to the women who waste their lives without ever understanding their own unhappiness. Trapped in suburbs whose cultural isolation had only just begun in 1913, when the poem was first published, the women's plight represented for Pound all the oppressiveness of a society which saw a wife as one of her husband's possessions, to be "bought" and controlled. The poem takes the form of an address by the poet to his songs, and the resulting emphasis on literature's power to reach those men and women suffering under society's oppressions is perfectly appropriate. For Pound the heart of the problem lies not in some conscious malevolence on the part of a few, but in "the tyranny of the unimaginative," and his desire is to pierce the ennui, to reach "those who have lost their interest." When he commands his poem to "defy opinion" he is acting out of his belief that the structures of social oppression have their origin in the mind, and that therefore they may be altered, as all imaginative structures may be, through the power of art to shape our perceptions.

In the composite portrait of social good and evil which Pound was creating in the short, satiric poems which constituted one aspect of *Lustra*, a broad range of attitudes is evident. In a poem such as "The Rest," for instance, America becomes overtly repressive, enslaving and breaking artists, who are pictured as "thwarted with systems,/Helpless against the control." They live in a hostile environment, "hated, shut in, mistrusted," trapped among bourgeois materialists who fear their truths, disdain beauty, and use "false knowledge" to preserve a closed society. In that poem, Pound presents himself as a successful expatriate and offers his encouragement to the "helpless few" who cannot escape. Elsewhere, his tone is less bitter, and he emphasizes specific kinds of social pretension—like that of the woman in "Albatre," whose posing is caught in one casual, but devasting, bit of description: "This lady in the white bathrobe which she calls a peignoir." In "Black Slippers: Bellotti" he describes a woman in a restaurant who has removed her "little suede slippers" and delicately put a napkin on the floor to protect her white stockings. The gesture, as well as her small talk, is pretentious, and Pound's satiric reduction is simply to watch her reenter her shoes, "with a groan."

Pound never wavered in his refusal to write a poetry easily accessible to the common reader, because that seemed to him a betrayal of the very integrity of imagination so desperately needed at the time. But while that would seem at first to be a rather aristocratic stance, Pound's fundamental identification was always with the people. His intuitions were those of a kind of romantic populist, as, for example, in "Salutation," where he addresses the "generation of the thoroughly smug" (and obviously upper class) to point out the far greater happiness and spontaneity of fishermen and their families, with their "smiles full of teeth" and their "ungainly laughter." The poet regards himself as somewhere in between the worker's simplicity and the rich man's ennui, and the poem's comic ending carries the hierarchy to its ultimate point of animal freedom in a lake full of fish that "do not even own clothing." The attenuated vitality of the upper classes is satirized again in "Les Millwins," where "the mauve and greenish souls of the little Millwins" are compared to limp, unused boas, as they attend a performance of the Russian Ballet. Amazed by the modernistic exuberance of Diaghilev's company and by the antics of the avant-garde art students in the audience, the Millwins can only look on "with their large and anaemic eyes." Pound's most direct satiric attack on the British aristocracy is "The Bellaires." In that poem he recounts the ultimate collapse of a great family's fortunes, in legal maneuvering, confusion, and finally the squire's retreat across the channel to the safety of exile in the south of France. The Bellaires are presented as totally incapable of intelligent action in the real world, as preserving their position solely through the entrenched power and influence of inherited wealth. Even when the money has gone, they are able to invoke the revered authority of tradition and established class superiority: the squire's stable of fine horses and hunting dogs—the anachronistic symbol of an older way of life, and totally useless to a man in bankruptcy—must not be seized by creditors because they descend from animals given to the Bellaires by medieval kings. And the family, useless and parasitic in living off the accomplishments of dead ancestors, attracts to itself an equally parasitic circle of lawyers, advisors, and hangers-on: "the sole result was bills/From lawyers to whom no one was indebted." Amusing as the poem is, the social implications of the picture it paints are ugly indeed, and Pound was deadly serious in his satire. These poems have probably received less critical attention than any of his other works, and to be sure, many of them are heavy-handed, especially when they are read along side the poems of *Cathay*. But Pound's commitment to social justice was growing steadily more important to the wholeness of his art. It was no hobby, no crank distraction from his lyric gift (as Noel Stock suggests in his biography),[3] and it first came to clear definition in these little poems of social satire.

II *Society in the Mirror of the Past*

In 1918 Pound published together two sequences of poems—"Moeurs Contemporaines" and "Langue d'Oc." The first was a series of sketches of men and women who might have been found in recent British society, while the second consisted of translations from the Provençal, evoking the very different social world of medieval France. Juxtaposed in the pages of the *Little Review*, they offered a further extension of Pound's poetic means of social criticism in their obvious contrast, requiring no additional comment. "Moeurs Contemporaines" presents a scene of human relationships taking place within a very refined, and very confining, fabric of social rules. The tone is reminiscent of Henry James (who is mentioned in one of the poems) in its attempt to reproduce a precise quality of feeling, both of individual emotion and social atmosphere. The characters Pound creates tend to be diminished in one way or another. Thus Mr. Hecatomb Styrax, in the first poem, is a member of the landed gentry who has a great many muscles and not much sense, who "does not believe in aesthetics," and who marries when he is twenty-eight (and still a virgin) only to drive his wife "from one religious excess to another" through his "ineptitudes." As a mountain climber and an anti-intellectual, he is an ideal member of the aristocracy, though even at the level of animal spirits his apparent robustness is flawed by sexual inadequacy.

The theme of sexuality, as an index of social and personal sanity, plays a principal role in the sequence. "Clara," for example, is a neurotic modern woman troubled by vague anxieties. At sixteen she had had a "distaste for caresses," and then grown up to two unhappy marriages, finally entering a convent where she "does not desire her children,/Or any more children." Suggesting a sexual basis for her troubles, Pound also notes that her mind remains uncultivated, and concludes with a portrait of a woman whose fears have incapacitated her for any kind of life at all: "Her ambition is vague and indefinite,/She will neither stay in nor come out." In similar fashion, section 4 offers a sketch of a man who to the world seems established as an officer and a gentleman, but who still, at the age of twenty-seven, remains a child to parents who do not even let him open his own mail. Another outwardly respectable member of the British establishment, his lack of sexual identity is emphasized by Pound, who refers to him by the sexless pronoun "its" and who defines his parents *only* by reference to their gender (e.g., "its maternal parent").

The poems of "Langue d'Oc" offer a striking contrast to these images of modern men and women paralyzed by repression and inadequacy. In Pound's notion that Provençal culture preserved some of the insights of the classical world, the ethic of love held a prominent place. Regarding their healthy valuation of love and sexuality as a central way to wisdom, and even a symbolic path to spiritual insight, Pound saw the Albigensian Crusade, which destroyed the culture of Provence, as in part the expression of a repressive, ascetic Christianity which was coming everywhere to prevail. But in the love poetry of the troubadours, a different world was still accessible, a world whose celebration of love was joyful and decisive. The "Langue d'Oc" poems all treat the situation of courtly love, each one assuming a particular voice and focusing on some part of the total experience. Part 2, for example, begins with a conventional generalization about spring, and then moves to the specific situation of the speaker, whose character has been much more sharply defined by the end of the poem than has the love plot in which he is involved. The preceding poem is more dramatic, set as it is at dawn outside the chamber of a lady whose lover has been with her all night. The voice of the lover's companion, standing watch outside, conveys a witty sense of exuberant, though dangerous, adventure. And the response from the lover inside (in a "bass voice") suggests all the manly conventions of the romantic hero:

> Wait, my good fellow. For such joy I take
> With her venust and noblest to my make
> To hold embracèd, and will not her forsake
> For yammer of the cuckold,
>   Though day break.

In "Descant on a Theme by Cerclamon," the dramatic moment gives way to a traditional lover's complaint. The poem is more leisurely and reflective in tone, moving through all the poetic conventions, from falling leaves which reflect the falling spirits of a disappointed lover, to a comparison of the beloved to the sun's glitter, to the lover's disease of "shake and burn and quiver." The poem is a graceful treatment of a traditional form, using the conventional exploration of feeling of the lover's complaint to create still another distinct sensibility.

Though the poems of "Langue d'Oc" are all slightly different in form, they are alike in two important ways. First, in exploring the qualities of specific moments of experience they project characters who are all, in their particular ways, vigorous, witty, decisive, joyful. There is none of the neurotic incapacity to live, and especially to love, that characterizes so many of the portraits in "Moeurs Contemporaines." And secondly, there was by implication a society in medieval Languedoc which sanctioned the sensual joys of love and natural beauty, celebrating them in a verse tradition which occupied an honored place in the culture.

It was a time when men and women were taught to know themselves as a part of that natural world from which the poets drew their countless images of birds, hail storm, and hawthorn bough. Poetry spoke openly about feelings of desire, aggression, and despair, and the conventions of a poetic tradition channeled those potentially frightening emotions in reassuring ways. By contrast, Pound's modern sequence seems to picture a time when men are so unable to deal with emotions like desire that they must either avoid them entirely, or yield to them entirely: the choice is abstinence or orgy, and in neither case is the rich, sensitive, humane experience of the troubadours possible. The people of "Moeurs Contemporaines" are all in various ways in retreat from a world which they do not want to know. Whether literally in a convent, or in the equally cloistered retreat of a twenty-seven-year-long childhood they all fear and avoid carnal knowledge, and that childish fear is generalized into an avoidance of any knowledge at all. The hostility, or at best lack of interest in any kind of learning, which the characters of Pound's sequence demonstrate, is only the defensive response of men and women who do not want to remember that "know" once had a sexual meaning. By 1918, Freud had already learned to take such connections seriously, and so in his studies of the troubadours, had Pound. Many years later, in canto 74, he distilled his insight in a simple phrase: "in coitu inluminatio" — coition maketh the light to shine.

III   *"Homage to Sextus Propertius"*

Sextus Propertius was a Roman poet who wrote about love, in the tradition of the Latin elegists, at the time of Virgil and Horace. In 1919, Pound brought out what appeared to be a translation of some of his *Elegies*, provoking an immediate controversy which has not yet been resolved. Typical of those who attacked the piece was William Hale, a professor of classics at the University of Chicago, who asserted in his review that "If Mr. Pound were a professor of Latin, there would be nothing left for him but suicide."[4] Hale's attack, and many of those which followed, was based on the assumption that Pound was attempting a literal translation of the Latin, and committing a great many blunders in the process. While Pound's version does follow the Latin quite closely at times, it is indeed likely to stray far from its model at others. But Pound, in defending himself against such charges, rejected their basic premise: "There was never any question of translation, let alone literal translation. My job was to bring a dead man to life."[5] Calling Hale "an example of why Latin poets are not read," Pound was all the more confirmed in his hatred for the pedantry and the diminished imagination of academic "authorities" who could not even recognize his "Homage" for what it was: a new poem in honor of an older poet whose themes, manner, tone, and language might be made relevant to our own age.

As Pound himself pointed out in a letter to one of his old professors,[6] he had included in his poem such anachronisms as a reference to Hesiod as "the ancient, respected Wordsworthian," and a parody of Yeats' style ("Sadness hung over the house, and the desolated female attendants/Were desolated because she had told them her dreams")—hardly the result of mistaken translation. Even today some critics still ignore Pound's accounts of his intention, and continue to regard him as a "scholar *manqué*" who was attempting a translation which was beyond his powers.[7] J. P. Sullivan, on the other hand, in his major study of "Homage," concludes that Pound did succeed in finding a language truer to the original than any of the earlier translations. He argues that Pound did revive interest in a poet who had been little read, except by specialists, and that just as Wai-lim Yip has demonstrated for the *Cathay* translations, Pound's sensitivity to poetic values sometimes enabled him to succeed in capturing the authentic quality of the original, where the most learned scholars had failed: "I have tried to avoid claiming for Pound any more extensive knowledge of Latin than he himself would claim. What can be claimed for him is an intuitive flair for language and in particular the language of poetry; it is this which has led him to the right language to express the sensibility he discerned in Propertius through the veils of a foreign, and in more significant ways *alien*, tongue."[8]

But beyond the question of accurate translation, intuitive or otherwise, Pound's claim for the contemporary relevancy of his work is important and ought to be taken seriously. In a letter to A. R. Orage[9] he described a figure he had thought of portraying which included not only Propertius himself, but "the spirit of the young man of the Augustan Age, hating rhetoric and undeceived by imperial hog-wash." And later, replying to Harriet Monroe's criticism, he wrote that the poem "presents certain emotions as vital to me in 1917, faced with the infinite and ineffable imbecility of the British Empire, as they were to Propertius some centuries earlier, when faced with the infinite and ineffable imbecility of the Roman Empire."[10] Writing during wartime, when artists and writers were being encouraged to lend their power over imagination to the policies of the government (following the example of men like Kipling), Pound felt a growing antipathy for any kind of propagandistic use of art, particularly in the service of a government which he disliked. He had always, of course, disapproved of rhetorical, public verse, like that of the Victorians, and his observation of the present only suggested that poets must continue to resist the persistent demand that they produce such "official" art. In the "Homage" he created a persona who embodies his conception of the artist who finds himself in opposition to his nation's pretensions. Pound's Propertius is a love poet who disdains the patriotic verse he has been asked to write, adopting a manner which is ironic and which achieves its most telling effects through the connotations of its diction. We should remember, for instance, that when Pound speaks, near the beginning of the poem, of "celebrities," a word which even in 1917 suggested newspaper gossip and crowds of fawning admirers, he is referring to heroes like Caesar, or the Aeneas of Virgil's epic. And to describe the glorious conquests of a victorious nation as "the distentions of Empire" is to evoke the familiar satiric cartoon of John Bull, grossly overstuffed with his beef and potatoes. Though never stated in so many words, the effect of such language is to reduce immortal reputation, the very stuff of epic poetry, to a level at which "Roman reputations" will more likely suggest the trivial desire to be recognized in public places.

Like *Cathay*, the "Homage to Sextus Propertius" must be read with at least some consciousness of the times in which it was written. Far more pointed in its social criticism than the simpler, elegiac translations from the Chinese, the "Homage" is not so much an account of the effects of war as it is the first step in a project which Pound later noted in the brief biography preceding his *Selected Poems:* "1918 began investigation of causes of war, to oppose same." For Pound's Propertius, the pretensions of empire are ridiculous, but as a poet his attack is directed primarily against the perversion of art into a means of publicizing and glorifying war. His tone is ironic, as it is, for example, in part 12 (*P*, 229), where he mocks the composition of the *Aeneid* by Virgil, his contemporary. Advising other authors to "make way," he refers to Virgil's poem as being "in the course of construction." The effect is to reduce a great epic, traditionally the loftiest of literary genres, to something like a new road or a public building, custom built to government specifications.

As a poem about the proper role of the artist in society, the "Homage" stands clearly against that poetry which offers only what the public has been taught to expect: "resonance, resonance and sonority . . . like a goose." But the elegiac note which had been predominant in *Cathay* is present here as well, in a strong sense of the transitory nature of the things of man: "Flame burns, rain sinks into the cracks/And they all go to rack ruin beneath the thud of the years." If the poem is an indirect account of the emotions which Pound felt as an artist confronted by increasingly outrageous imperial foolishness, it is also a continuation of some of his older poetic interests. As one of Pound's "major personae," Propertius is defined, in the context of his love affair with Cynthia, in some detail. Pound is able to explore a range of emotion which had not been possible in shorter poems, moving from the satiric note of his criticism of "political poems" to feelings of genuine passion, sadness, and anger. Section 4, for example, presents a discussion between Propertius and his slave, Lydgamus, in which Lydgamus reports the exaggerated sorrow and recriminations of Cynthia upon learning that Propertius had declined to come to her late at night, after she had sent for him. Propertius, however, suspects that she has betrayed him with Lydgamus himself, and refuses to believe the account of her grief. The dramatic situation thus makes the discussion which is the poem's focus very complex and ironic. Pound captures a tone in Propertius' speech which, in its ironic parody of Cynthia's supposed grief, expresses all the anger and frustration he feels about her and about his dependence on a suspect messenger:

> Damp woolly handkerchiefs were stuffed into her undryable eyes,
> And a querulous noise responded to our solicitous reprobations.
> For which things you will get a reward from me, Lydgamus?
> To say many things is equal to having a home.

More fully dramatic than most of the poetic situations which
Pound uses to reveal emotion, this section is complemented by
other, more reflective parts of the poem. Whatever the degree
of drama, though, the exploration of feeling is one of the poem's
continuing concerns.

This is not to say that Pound's exploration of Propertius' love
for Cynthia is merely the dramatic occasion for a poem about
states of feeling. Extended dramatic monologue, and satiric
critique of imperial culture, the "Homage" is also a vision of
truths not to be found in power and political reputation. J. P.
Sullivan, contrasting Pound and Eliot, has said that "Pound is not
concerned with any deeper spiritual reality; his roots strike only
into this world and this society and it is here that he wishes
reform to begin."[11] Pound is indeed concerned with changing a
society destructive of human values, but to say that his interests
are *only* social and worldly is simply to ignore a visionary quest in
his work which dates from his earliest poems and which
penetrates the veil of nature more deeply than any of Eliot's
discourses on mystical doctrine. In the "Homage," that quest is
manifest in poetry which celebrates the love of man and woman:

> And in the mean time my songs will travel,
> And the devirginated young ladies will enjoy them
>   when they have got over the strangeness,
> For Orpheus tamed the wild beasts —
>   and held up the Threician river. . . .

In lines which illustrate an ironic mockery of society's conventional expectations which is one of the poem's aspects, Pound
also defines the shape of his positive vision. In the *Cantos* he
assumes the persona of Odysseus, descending into hell to begin a
journey through history in search of that pattern of nature's
wholeness which our world of greed and hate has lost. In
"Homage to Sextus Propertius" he used a different figure, but
the shape of his quest was clear already. "Orfeo" is the name
Pound chose for an epigraph, and like Odysseus, Orpheus was a
man who descended into the underworld. He made his journey
out of love for Eurydice, and though he lost her to the darkness
which always prevails, he became one with the deepest
harmonies of nature, speaking through his song to every plant
and animal, and even to the stones. For Pound, who had already

written, in "Psychology and Troubadours," of a "germinal universe of wood alive, of stone alive," and whose early poems were filled with the light-giving ladies of Provençal tradition, Orpheus was a fitting model for his Propertius, who would follow his own unfaithful lady through a kind of hell. And like the legendary Orpheus, who taught the arts of peace to the warlike people of Thrace, Propertius sees the lesson of nature, that "long night comes upon you/and a day when no day returns," and he too has his truth to teach. In the "Homage to Sextus Propertius," Pound achieves a more inclusive poetry, bringing together his bitter rejection of the rhetoric of empire, and his vision of an art dedicated to the private truth which that rhetoric must always try to repress: the truth of lives lived in acceptance of nature's flow, driving toward death, mocking Caesar.

CHAPTER 6

Toward a Major Form

I   *"Near Perigord"*

P OUND'S imagist verse had served to free him from many of
the restrictions of an older tradition which was still present in
much of his early work. He had found in imagism a new economy
and precision of statement, and a faith in the communicative
power of simple poetic images which enabled him to abandon
the rhetoric which he had always hated, as well as the "softness"
of the Celtic twilight, which he was growing to hate. In his
theory of the image, Pound had suggested that a great deal of
knowledge and feeling might be focused in a moment's space,
but the generally brief imagist poems which issued from the
theory offered little means of dealing with large or complicated
aspects of reality. Pound saw the restrictions of his form all too
clearly in the trivial "imagist" poems of some of his imitators, and
he saw those restrictions just as he was becoming more vitally
concerned to write a poetry capable of illuminating the follies of
a shallow, unjust, materialistic society. The satiric poems of
Lustra were a first attempt to explore such content, but they
could not offer the sort of extended vision which was necessary
for a poet who knew that society is not a conglomeration of
separate acts of virtue or vice, but a complex, interrelated
pattern. Pound's need was to find a way to extend his imagist
principles into a technique capable of treating the inclusive and
the complex without sacrificing any of the economy or the
intense fusion of thought and feeling which he had claimed for
the image.

The demands of a poetry of social criticism, however, were not
alone responsible for Pound's exploration of new forms beyond

imagism. The shape of society concerned him greatly, but he did not isolate that topic from his other interests, and in fact he saw it all as of a piece—social custom, public ethics, art, the uniqueness of individual experience. The reality we know involves all of those things, and all of them interact with one another. As early as 1915 he had begun to extend his imagist methods in poems which confronted the complexity of that reality. "Villanelle: The Psychological Hour," for example, is a poem about the loneliness and self-doubt of a middle-aged poet whose invitation to visit has apparently been ignored by two new "friends." Essentially a dramatic monologue, the poem consists primarily in its character's reflections and while his thoughts are reasonably coherent, they are not entirely so. There is no pattern of logical argument, as thought follows thought in a reverie which serves to reveal psychological reality, and the poem's force really consists in a few "luminous details": books overcarefully arranged before the expected visit, the poet (Prufrock-like) watching "the rain, the wandering buses" from his window, the terseness of "another man's note" which focuses all the poet's feelings of rejection and isolation—"Dear Pound, I am leaving England." Though in some ways this poem seems little different from Pound's earlier dramatic monologues, it carries his practice of providing little explanation of "plot" still further, and it takes full advantage of the suggestive power of a few carefully chosen images.

As preparation for the innovative form of *The Cantos*, however, "Villanelle: The Psychological Hour" was far less significant than the poem which appeared with it in the December, 1915, issue of *Poetry*. "Near Perigord" was Pound's last poem about Bertran de Born, and written as he was beginning work on the earliest cantos, it reveals a form which mirrors Pound's vision of the complexity of experience in language of imagist clarity. As Louis Kampf has observed with regard to the temper of art in the twentieth century, "doubts about the foundations of knowledge have had a decisive influence on—no, have forced in entirely new directions—the forms of our arts, sciences, and modes of action. And no amount of reasoning, in whatever directions, is likely to still our doubts."[1] While Pound never shared the radical doubt which led so many of his contemporaries to an existential vision of man's isolation in a world he cannot know, Pound's faith in the possibility of knowing truly was not based on any ignorance, or willful ignoring, of the drift of modern thought. He too saw the limits of mind—particularly in its fondness for a logical discourse which distorts the very reality it seems to treat so objectively. And he also knew how very difficult it is to see into the private experience of another human being. The ambiguity and the opacity of a life not his own was Pound's subject in "Near Perigord," and his task was made all the more difficult by the fact that the man he would know had been dead for seven hundred years.

In his previous poems concerning Bertran de Born, Pound had offered a very great range of portraits: the bloodthirsty warrior of "Sestina: Altaforte," the sensitive elegiac poet of "Planh for the Young English King," and the witty lover of "Na Audiart." In "Near Perigord" he brought those conflicting facets of a life together into a single poem, underlining the problematic nature of all our attempts to reconstruct the past. The poem focuses on Bertran's love for the lady Maent, and on his motive in that love. On the one hand, there is the evidence of his canzone ("Dompna Pois de me No'us Cal"), in which he pleads his lover's case through the conceit of an ideal lady, assembled in imagination out of the perfections of many other ladies, and yet failing to rival Maent. But Bertran was also known for the violent acts and the scheming which led Dante to place him in the *Inferno* as a "stirrer-up of strife." Pound mentions his reputation as one "who set the strife between brother and brother," and he suggests that Bertran's motive for making such trouble was simply political. Surrounded by stronger enemies, his only chance for survival was to set them against each other, to "stir old grudges" and so hope to live by such scheming. From this point of view, Bertran's wooing of the lady Maent is simply the devious plot of a man maneuvering to strengthen his political position, and Pound's tone reflects the cynicism of such a view: "He loved this lady in castle Montagnac?/The castle flanked him—he had need of it."

Having posed the terms of a seemingly insoluble puzzle, Pound begins the second part of the poem with a statement which is not simply ironic: "End fact. Try fiction." Although part 1 seems anything but "fact," Pound would have us understand that the most "objective" account of history can really offer no more certainty than this record of conflicting, mysterious bits of old writing and old reputation. His attitude toward the task of recreating the past is already like that of the ancient Chinese historians, praised by Confucius in canto 13, who "left blanks in their writings,/I mean for things they didn't know." In part 2, he abandons the tone of the historian weighing his fragmentary facts, and assumes instead the mode of imagination, picturing a red-bearded Bertran struggling with his rhymes, and sending his jongleur off to sing them. Pound imagines Bertran's scheme, coded in poetry, carried through the courts until Arrimon Luc D'Esparo suddenly sees its hidden meaning and informs Richard Coeur de Lion, Bertran's enemy. Equally plausible, this fictive account is still no more certain than the "factual" one had been, and Pound emphasizes its problematic quality. He describes Bertran caught and "smoked out," and then, reversing the drift of his speculation, suggests that Bertran might just as well have escaped, and "prospered." The fiction culminates in a conversation between Richard and Arnaut Daniel, years after Bertran has been finally defeated. Neither soldier nor poet is able to say anything certain about the man, and in their exchange, Pound catches all the difficulty of ever resolving so puzzling a riddle: "'You knew the man.'/'*You* knew the man.'" The point is that neither man knew him wholly, and when Pound ends the section by quoting Dante's account, the effect is to call even that most famous bit of evidence into question.

In the poem's final section, Pound shifts to Bertran's own point of view, as he struggles to understand Maent, who is just as puzzling as he is himself. The passage begins lyrically, "in the young days when the deep sky befriended," suggesting that their love was genuine. But a bit of remembered dialogue reveals strife and misunderstanding between them as well, and the poem ends as Bertran confronts the fact that she is gone, "untouched, unreachable," and that she must always remain a mystery to him, "a shifting change,/A broken bundle of mirrors." "Near Perigord" is in the tradition of Pound's earlier poems after Browning, and like them it evokes a unique personality and a distinct sense of a time long past. But it also reveals a view of how we might know that past which was changing in very significant ways. In setting out to apprehend the reality of history, Pound had come to reject almost entirely the coherent, synthetic—and distorting—approach of the traditional historian, turning instead to that jumble of bits and pieces of fact (which is all we ever had to work with) in search of those "luminous details" which offer as much genuine insight as we can hope to find—and without the illusion of wholeness where none is possible. In his search for a way to communicate that new apprehension of the past, Pound had already begun to move toward radical innovation in poetic form, letting his poem assume the shape of history as he had come increasingly to see it: a pattern of images which might be juxtaposed in very illuminating ways, but which could not be subsumed into any larger framework of coherent narrative, or philosophical discourse, or psychological explanation.

II   Hugh Selwyn Mauberley: *Social Critique*

Pound's discontent with British society, and particularly with what he considered to be the low valuation of serious art in that society, had been growing stronger during the years of World War I. By 1920 he was ready to leave England, and late in that year he and his wife chose Paris as their new home. He had been voicing his criticisms for some years, in the short satiric poems of *Lustra,* and more fully, in the "Homage to Sextus Propertius," where he had opposed the pretensions of an imperialist state which would force art to serve the "public good," rather than its own concern with beauty, and love, and the private experience of our mortality. It was also during those years of heightening social consciousness, that Pound came to question the older forms of his poetry, accepting finally what men like Wyndham Lewis had been urging for years—the necessity of shaping the form of his verse in radically new ways, a task already taken for granted by the plastic arts. In 1920 he published a long poem which carried his earlier, tentative, stylistic innovations to a much more fully realized point. *Hugh Selwyn Mauberley* was not only his first experiment in a thoroughly modernist style, but it spoke decisively to the larger social concerns which had gradually been leading him to break with his own past.

In his footnote to the poem, Pound calls it "a farewell to London," and it is that, in a number of ways. The poem's hero is yet another persona, though in this case he is a persona who represents much of what Pound himself had been during his years in London. As John Espey demonstrated most clearly,[2] the poem's chief action is the gradual separation of Pound, about to leave England for a new country and a radically altered poetic task, from that persona—a part of himself, but a part he had chosen to leave behind. Appropriately, the poem opens with a kind of epitaph, a judgment on the poetic career of "E. P.," in a voice which is not entirely unsympathetic, but which does preserve its ironic distance as it dismisses its subject as a failure, a rather foolish tilter-at-windmills. This was the poet who had set out to begin a new renaissance, a cultural vortex which might have drawn on the imaginative resources of a world far wider than that of Europe in the fifteenth century. But by the end of the war which destroyed so many idealistic hopes, he knew he had misjudged a public totally in the hands of those whose business it was to sell art for profit. "Out of key with his time," E. P.'s struggle had been an impossible one, even though right and worthy, and the poem's metaphors emphasize Pound's ambivalence—he is pictured as a yokel, "out of date," as ridiculously laboring to wring lilies from an acorn, as a doomed hero battling the gods, as a fish fooled by an artificial fly. Comparing himself to a stopped Odysseus, Pound replaces Penelope, as the object of his quest, with Flaubert, whose precise, economical style had possessed an integrity which Pound used as model for his imagist rule that poetry should be at least as well written as prose. Acknowledging his failure to make that standard general among writers more concerned with the easy clichés of popular taste, however, he paraphrases the opening of François Villon's *Le Testament*, an allusion which links his own alienation to that of another poet who wrote in defiance of the accepted canons of his time. Pound had once called Villon "a voice of suffering, of mockery, of irrevocable fact,"[3] and as he saw the impossibility of dislodging the arbiters of public taste, he was all the more drawn to the role of the artist who continues in exile to speak the needful truth, who, like Villon, "never lies to himself."

After the opening section, with its allusiveness and its distanced, ironic tone, Pound turns to a more direct attack on the evils of the society he is about to leave. Through the next four sections he numbers the follies of a culture too cheapened to see the possibility of its own rebirth. In part 2, for example, he denounces contemporary artistic values as pandering to a public taste which would have nothing more challenging than a reflection of its own self-image, certainly not a classical beauty nor "the obscure reveries" of a poetry of introspection. Preferring "mendacities" to "the classics in paraphrase," this is the society which had refused to recognize Pound's "Homage to

Sextus Propertius" as an attempt to make the poetry of a distant age live again for the present. It is a society debased by the expectations of a mass-produced taste which prefers molded plaster to the precise craftsmanship of classical sculpture. Pound saw the *genuine* needs of his age as far different from those superficial "demands" of a public which had been conditioned, by the increasingly pervasive values of its own technology, to accept shoddy merchandise. Pound's critique of a situation in which human values had been subordinated to the requirements of technology and profit was not the romantic nostalgia of another proponent of village crafts, but an analysis of what has come to be recognized as a crucial force in the shaping of our human environment. Writing about "The City" several years later, Pound rejected the notion (which he ascribed to Thomas Edison) that scientific "advancement," rather than human need, should determine the shape of future cities.[4]

The thrust of Pound's argument was the same as it had been fifteen years earlier in *Patria Mia:* "The first duty of a nation is to conserve its human resources."[5] When, in part 3 of *Mauberley,* he deplores our diminished modern world, in which the "pianola" and its harsh, mechanical music, has replaced the classic beauty of Sappho's lute, he places that aesthetic loss in a context which ultimately reveals its deeper human consequences. The outward manifestation of our new pattern of culture may be seen in the quick, profitable turnover of cheap goods which has destroyed the older sense of lasting beauty. Heraclitus' belief that the world is essentially in a state of endless change has been reinterpreted, in economic terms, as a vision of shoddy mass production. It is an age when the Beautiful ("Τò Καλσν") is "decreed in the market place," and when neither genuine sensuality ("faun's flesh") nor spiritual awareness ("Saint's vision") is available to shape the conduct of our lives. Lacking these fundamentally human bases of experience, men and women are forced to rely on popular democracy and the popular press to guide the ordering of their society. And yet both press and politics are subject to the laws of a marketplace which has come to value profit more than human resources, with the result that the people have neither access to knowledge nor to decent government. Equal only "in law," we "choose a knave or an eunuch/To rule over us."

Although Pound had abandoned any continuous thread of

narrative or rhetorical structure to unite these stanzas, his thought was far more coherent than many readers have understood. If the poem's surface is discontinuous, it nevertheless does fall into clearly meaningful patterns, and so with the poem's argument. Pound does not offer a syllogistic analysis of the evils of modern society, but he does set down a series of details which gradually define the shape of the social process he would make us see. Thus he moves from the debased aesthetic values of part 2, to the portrait in part 3 of the way in which a cheap marketplace ethic can act to block our access to information, to spiritual insight, and even to our own bodies, so that society no longer serves genuinely human ends. For Pound, that growing disdain for human resources stands as direct cause to the effect he pictures in parts 4 and 5: young men fighting a worthless war for the sake of old men who lie, and grow rich, protected by the patriotic illusions of their countrymen. World War I, wasting lives on a scale never seen before, was profoundly disturbing to an entire generation of European artists, but to Pound it seemed less an unspeakable, mysterious calamity than the logical consequence of society's recent patterns. Pound knew that a society is of one piece, that lying for profit in the marketplace cannot be separated from lying for profit in politics, and that war is only the most extreme expression of society's disregard for human values.

In his attempt to understand the social forces which had led to such destruction, Pound had begun to look increasingly to economic factors. Unorthodox monetary theories were very much in the air during the years following the First World War, and in the same year that *Hugh Selwyn Mauberley* was published, Pound reviewed the work of one theorist, Major C. H. Douglas, calling his ideas "a new and definite force in economic thought, and, moreover, . . . a force well employed and well directed, that is to say directed toward a more humane standard of life; directed to the prevention of new wars, wars blown up out of economic villanies at the whim and instigation of small bodies of irresponsible individuals."[6] If the war had been deadly evidence of the corruption of European society, it did not really cause a fundamental change of view for Pound, who had already been calling for a new renaissance for nearly a decade. In his eyes, the cultural vitality which had encouraged men and women in medieval Provence and Renaissance Italy to know themselves fully in the context of a world alive and full of meaning, had been eroding for centuries. The dead stuff of later painting—clothes and furniture and human bodies devoid of any sign of animating spirit—seemed to him the product of a world unable to see beyond matter itself. Bereft of the power to know his "kinship to the vital universe, to the tree and the living rock,"[7] modern man was the victim of a culture which had taught him to forget that truth, to live instead in the prideful exploitation of nature and of other men and women. The war was simply the last tragic manifestation of a spent culture:

> Charm, smiling at the good mouth,
> Quick eyes gone under earth's lid,
>
> For two gross of broken statues,
> For a few thousand battered books.

III   *Mauberley: the artist in opposition*

In *Patria Mia,* Pound had written that "So far as I can make out, there is no morality in England which is not in one way or another a manifestation of the sense of property."[8] Pound was not alone in making such an assessment of what, for many, seemed to be the central heritage of Victorian England. Throughout the nineteenth century there had been a persistent current of opposition (though out of the mainstream, to be sure) against the prevailing faith in material progress. That opposition became more pronounced as the century advanced, culminating in the Pre-Raphaelite and later "aesthetic" movements which cultivated a beauty visionary rather than materialistic, and which flaunted their private morality against what seemed hypocritical repressiveness in the Victorian ethic. Early in his career Pound had identified himself strongly with those poets— Swinburne and Rossetti, Dowson, Johnson, and most of all, the young W. B. Yeats. His allegiance to their artistic values had been the first step in dissociating himself from the society which, by 1920, seemed to have brought about its own destruction. And when he turned, in *Hugh Selwyn Mauberley,* from the desolation and wastage of the war in section 5 to "Yeux Glauques," he was returning in part to the history of his own search for the artist's proper role in a time when he could share few of the assumptions of his society.

Simply put, "Yeux Glauques" is a survey of the sort of process which had occurred as artists began to speak against the "official" arbiters of Victorian aesthetic value. The politician Gladstone had been respected while Swinburne and Rossetti were "still abused." Edward Fitzgerald published his translation of *The Rubáiyát of Omar Khayyám*, only to have it ignored for many years by a public trained to expect more enlightening fare. Painters such as Sir Edward Burne-Jones, in his painting *King Cophetua and the Beggar Maid*, strove to evoke a mysterious beauty, while the spokesmen for official canons of taste attacked the supposed immorality of such art. R. W. Buchanan had attacked a poem of Rossetti's about a prostitute ("Jenny"), and his attitude seemed typical to Pound of the stony insensitivity which confronted those who had tried to recall Victorian England to truths forgotten in the rush to amass saleable goods.

If Pound had begun his career as a poet with the example of the nineties in mind, however, he ultimately came to see the failure, and even the danger, of that model. The poets of the old Rhymers' Club had rejected the shallow materialism of their age, but by 1915 Pound was forced to conclude that they had "chiefly gone out because of their muzziness, because of a softness derived, I think, not from books but from impressionist painting. They riot with half decayed fruit."[9] In "Sienna Mi Fe; Disfecemi Maremma," Pound acknowledged the failure of the nineties. Pound's Monsieur Verog was Victor Plarr, once a member of the Rhymers' Club, and now forgotten in his obscure position as librarian at the Royal College of Surgeons. The tone of this section is deliberately reflective, suggesting anecdotes told by a man recalling an age long dead. In keeping with his imagist principles, Pound offers none of the narrative content of those anecdotes, but the few details he does choose are sufficiently luminous. Lionel Johnson was said to have died by falling off a stool in a pub, while Ernest Dowson is pictured as living in the bohemian poverty of artistic alienation. Pound makes their weakness for alcohol clear, and in characterizing Selwyn Image (another member of the Rhymers' Club) as equally enamored of drink, dance, and religion, he undercuts the seriousness of the example they might offer to younger artists. The effect is to portray a movement which began in admirable opposition to the evils of its culture, but which quickly foundered in its own predeliction for a private, even self-indulgent pursuit of beauty, unsupported by any concern to right the public wrongs of the age. M. Verog lives on, but he lives "out of step with the decade," in a world of his own reveries, unable to communicate with those about to take up the struggle which he and his contemporaries had begun.

Through the next five sections, Pound turns from that failed movement of the late nineteenth century to examine the present prospects for an artist who would offer some viable alternative to the moral bankruptcy of his age. In a series of brief sketches he presents a very discouraging picture of the current London world of letters. "Brennbaum," for example, begins the sequence by portraying a man who has suppressed truths which should be basic to his being, in order to accept the easy respectability of society's conventions. Brennbaum is a Jew,[10] who knows the suffering and the alienation of his heritage—an exile endured in the belief that physical comfort, and even life itself, must be sacrificed to the transcendent reality of a higher destiny. Those "heavy memories of Horeb, Sinai and the forty years," however, are buried beneath an exterior manner which betrays no sign of moral struggle or divine vision. Dressed in upper-class correctness and looking on the world through "sky-like limpid eyes," Brennbaum seems untouched by the fact that he has betrayed his own heritage. But the memories are there nevertheless, though apparent only when the proper light falls across his face, and in describing his "stiffness from spats to collar/Never relaxing into grace," Pound suggests that he has bought his social position at heavy cost.

If Brennbaum represents a man willing to forsake the visionary heritage of Moses which even his name (which means "burning tree") suggests, "Mr. Nixon" is the man who would sell his artistic integrity for money. As a model of the commercially successful writer, Mr. Nixon's chief goal seems to have been to attain the "cream gilded cabin of his steam yacht"—a detail which defines the extent of his visions. Drawing on the dramatic lyric, Pound creates a speech which reveals both the aesthetic and the ethical conclusions which follow from a materialistic world view such as Mr. Nixon's. Given his emphasis on money as the chief good, literary value must be judged accordingly, and since poetry is not lucrative it should not be highly esteemed: "There's nothing in it." Even writing a column is a worthier task if it can accomplish the crucial goal of building a reputation. Nor are Mr. Nixon's aesthetic judgments free of more general ethical implications. In advising the young poet to "butter reviewers" and never to mention another writer without the prospect of boosting his own sales, he displays a willingness to place profit before the integrity of his language. For Pound in the *Cantos*, however, the need to "call things by their right names" would seem centrally important to any social reform, just as it did to many writers in the twenties, disillusioned by the empty rhetoric of World War I (e.g., Hemingway's hero, in *A Farewell to Arms*, who watches with disgust as yet another hypocritical proclamation is posted up).

If Mr. Nixon's conclusion was detestable, his historical observation was all too true, and part 10 is a further elaboration of that fact. Perhaps modeled after Ford Maddox Ford, as Hugh Kenner has suggested, this sketch describes a "stylist" who is precisely the opposite of Mr. Nixon. Rejecting the search for fame and money, he lives in the simple poverty of a country cottage with a leaky roof, practicing his craft without regard for how well his works will sell. In statements such as "Nature receives him," and "the soil meets his distress," Pound suggests that he has remained in touch with a living world long ago forgotten by the entrepreneurs of literary London. And yet there is the distinct sense that this stylist, writing with a craftsmanlike integrity out of his own private experience—like the ill-fated poets of the nineties—has, like them, become *too* private, choosing a way that might be called escapist. He is described as having "taken shelter" in a "haven from sophistications and contentions," and he lives with a mistress who is "placid and uneducated." Although his way is far more admirable than that of Mr. Nixon, it too is essentially a response to the debacle of the old aestheticism. Though refusing to give up the ideals of that movement, the stylist has retreated to a life so private that the honesty of his art can be of no use to the larger society which badly needs it.

Having established the two unacceptable extremes apparently available to the contemporary artist—in either pandering to society's values or ignoring them completely—Pound widens his scrutiny in the next two sections to include the social context of art. In part 11 he deals with a typical modern woman living in a suburb of London with a husband who is "the most bank-clerkly of Englishmen." Recalling a phrase from Remy de Gourmont, who had spoken of women as the conservators of Milesian traditions (referring to the erotic Greek *Milesian Tales)* Pound questions Gourmont's judgment, at least with regard to this woman who is so totally ruled by what "would fit her station." Pound's irony reduces "instinct," with all its suggestion of deeply rooted biological drives, to the level of table manners, learned or unlearned according to what a grandmother considers to be socially proper. For such a woman not only sexual behavior, but even sexual instinct itself has been made subject to what others have taught her about the conventions of society.

In part 12 Pound carries that motif further as he pictures an elegant literary salon whose proprietress evidently reserves her passion for men rich or tasteful enough to be able to dress well. Again, his irony is heavy in this sketch of a woman who is entirely at the mercy of the changing surface of her culture, in personal relationships as well as her understanding of art. If passion depends on the cut of a suit coat, poetry too has been reduced to a device for making time in high society, and in the extreme case of revolution, it might even prove useful as a "possible friend and comforter." In the social circle which Pound describes, the artist is one more participant in the struggle for place in a hierarchy based on birth, money, and a complex etiquette. And poetry is valued only insofar as it can be useful to that struggle—providing a quote, for example, to impress the Lady Jane. As he had done in part 9, Pound closes this section by changing the scene in the last two stanzas, offering a contrast which reminds us that his topic is the present state of our culture. He refers to Dr. Samuel Johnson and then to the Greek poetess, Sappho, and he contrasts the powerful integrity of their work with the modern degradation of art into merchandise to be sold for profit. The literary vitality of Dr. Johnson's Fleet Street has been obliterated by the "sale of half-hose," as the press has become less a medium for serious writing than simply a medium for advertising.

Through these first twelve sections, Pound has described a culture dominated by property and by a system of conventions which has undermined some of the most fundamental aspects of human experience. Superficial, repressed, and materialistic, it is a culture which allows little place for art, and as a context for the sort of artistic renascence which Pound had hoped to begin it only confirms the dreary judgment of the poem's first stanza: "wrong from the start." E. P. had hoped to confront the failures of his diminished age by regaining access to vital traditions too long lost. But that dream was blocked by the crassness of a "Mr. Nixon," the ineffective retreat of a "stylist," the superficiality of a "Lady Valentine," and the "Envoi" which ends the first half of the poem stands as evidence of how difficult it is to recover the vitality of those old traditions. Beginning with an echo of Edmund Waller's "Goe Lovely Rose," the "Envoi" is a poem in the manner of the Elizabethan lyric of love and mortality. Masterful in sound and rhythm, it demonstrates E. P.'s ability to draw on Renaissance conventions of language and metaphor. And yet, the result is finally irrelevant to the needs of the age. As created object it is admirable, and as evidence of the artistic vision of past eras it is convincing, but as a response to the condition of Europe after the Great War it fails to escape its own inspiration, to make the past new. To persist in such a direction would be to indulge in escapism like that of the nineties, or like that which Ford had identified when he rolled on the floor in derision at the archaic diction of the young Pound.

At this point in the sequence the figure of Mauberley takes on a quality which is at once more narrowly defined, and more clearly distinguished from Pound himself. As Pound notes, the poem is a "farewell to London," a turning away not only from a city but from an artistic role which Mauberley continues to play in the poem's concluding sections. Mauberley's art is characterized chiefly by its limitation, and when Pound quotes from the first poem in the sequence ("His true Penelope/Was Flaubert") his quotation marks underline the ironic fact that what had been a commitment to a craftsman's integrity in the pursuit of dangerous visions has been reduced to a concern for craft alone, and that craft a minor one. Limiting his aspirations to the "colourless" art of engraving, an "art in profile" which cannot deal with "the full smile," Mauberley appears unlikely to "forge Achaia."

The most critical point in the delineation of Mauberley's character, however, occurs in part 2. Certainly the most dense and allusive section of the poem, it also draws most fully on the techniques of stylistic distortion to suggest the nature of Mauberley's plight:

> Drifted . . . drifted precipitate,
> Asking time to be rid of . . .
> Of his bewilderment; to designate
> His new found orchid. . . .

Just as the language of these stanzas seems to be coming apart, so Mauberley drifts without apparent direction, confused and tentative. His artistic goal had been to produce a "series/Of curious heads in medallion," and in describing that very limited aim, Pound sees in Mauberley one of the central failings of our modern culture:

> —Given that is his "fundamental passion,"
> This urge to convey the relation
> Of eye-lid and cheek-bone
> By verbal manifestation. . . .

As a technical quality of modern verse that verbal precision is exactly what Pound had sought as an antidote to the rhetorical softness of the nineteenth century. But for Mauberley, what would have been commendable as method had itself become goal, and in applying terms such as "fundamental passion" and "urge" to Mauberley's rather trivial aims Pound was ironically pointing out the modern failure of vitality, and especially sexual vitality, which he had treated in "Moeurs Contemporaines." The neurotic indecision which that earlier sequence treated had been set against the Provence of "Langue d'Oc," with its living tradition of song rooted in the *genuinely* fundamental passions of human experience, and honored by a society which had not yet learned to see art as merchandise. Playing on the Greek root of orchid ("testicle"), Pound draws a poet who could regard the sexual invitation of a woman's eyes as no more than a technical challenge for his art. Mauberley had suffered a kind of "anaesthesis" of emotions so vital to the poet that Pound had once described them as the basis for an entire tradition of medieval visionary poetry. By the time he awoke to the demands of Eros, however, they were only possible in "retrospect."

In the final sections of "Mauberley" Pound simply records the inconsequential end of a poet trapped in the same pointless private triviality which had destroyed the nineties. Unconcerned with questions of social reform, he defends himself against the rigors of the real world by "constant elimination," simply excluding all disturbing elements from his consciousness until finally only consciousness itself is left. "Incapable of the least utterance or composition" even his desire for survival fades as he ends in a South Seas of his own imagination, contemplating tenuous images of beauty and failed as a man, a poet, and a mind responsible to other men and women. His only work is the "Medallion" which closes the sequence, and its exquisite portrait is finally rather chilling as it seems to freeze life itself beneath its amber glaze.

Pound was a poet deeply influenced by the past, and he had always been concerned to know how the past might be used, how it could be made new. In *Hugh Selwyn Mauberley* he recorded a decision reached only after painful years of poetic practice, self-criticism, and growing commitment to the social responsibility of art. The aestheticism of the nineties had been Pound's earliest model as a poet, but the solipsism of that movement could hold no promise in 1920 for a man who was still at heart an American populist, and who had lost dear friends to a war whose only point seemed to have been to make a few men rich, at the expense of many poor men dead. When Pound left London he was ready to commit himself to a new kind of poetry.

CHAPTER 7

The Cantos

I *Form*

*H*UGH *Selwyn Mauberley* was Pound's final separation from an age that was finished. Its subject was a failed poet, a man who had never been able to escape the narrow aestheticism with which Pound himself had begun. But if the poem's subject was the past gradually being cast off, its form was already anticipating the future in its achievement of a shifting, discontinuous style which leads directly into *The Cantos.* The poem was Pound's "farewell to London," and by December, 1920, he and his wife had indeed left England for good, moving to Paris, and then, for the winter months, to the Riviera. On arriving in Paris he explained his move to a newspaper interviewer by saying that he had found "the decay of the British Empire too depressing a spectacle to witness at close range."[1] Disgusted by a society whose imaginative power seemed to be spent, and confronted by increasing hostility to his own artistic programs, Pound came to Paris with the hope, shared by many at the time, that there he would find the sort of vital, cosmopolitan center for creative activity which he had once envisioned for one or two American cities. He came with the general shape of his new poetry clearly in mind, and already achieved in part in the structure of *Mauberley.* But even with its lack of narrative frame, its rich allusiveness, and its discontinuous surface, *Mauberley* was, finally, a closed, coherent portrait of a life.

The Cantos would carry Pound's experiments in form much farther, and as early as 1915, five years before the publication of *Mauberley,* he had begun work on them. In 1917 three cantos were published in *Poetry,* though Pound became dissatisfied with them almost immediately, and continued to revise and rearrange. The form of his new poems raised immediate objection from his contemporary readers, and the difficulties faced by anyone coming to *The Cantos* for the first time are just as great today. *The Cantos* are long—800 pages—and they are filled with a forbidding array of languages, styles, and seemingly cryptic allusions. The old discursive framework of nineteenth-century rhetoric, which Pound had been struggling to abandon almost from the start of his career, has been destroyed, leaving a vast mosaic of images and little obvious guidance as to how they are to be related into meaningful patterns. Not least among the problems a new reader faces is the formidable mass of scholarly commentary on the *Cantos*. Given the nature of the poem, much of this scholarship has understandably been devoted to identifying references, exploring Pound's sources, and examining very limited themes within the poem. As some critics have begun to note, the result of all this is that "the student often finds the text of the poem buried under mounds of scholarship whose relevance is frequently questionable and whose very presence sets up the most formidable of barriers between Pound and the would-be reader."[2] From the correspondence of John Adams and Thomas Jefferson, to Chinese history, to the Italian Renaissance, to modern theories of monetary reform, Pound provides countless starting points for inquiries so long and detailed that critics too often lose sight of the poem they had set out to understand.

But if *The Cantos* are difficult poetry, they are by no means inaccessible. Although many of the poem's details have yet to be fully explained, its poetic methods and its major concerns are clear enough. To some extent, all of Pound's readers have accepted the fact that much of what they encounter in the poem may not be familiar immediately, and may even remain opaque, but for most readers the only real prerequisite to reading is simply some sense of the poem's larger shape, of how so many disparate elements might somehow be seen to cohere. One early reader, puzzled by the poem's lack of apparent order, was William Butler Yeats, who offered this account of Pound's formal scheme: "Now at last he explains that it will, when the hundredth canto is finished, display a structure like that of a Bach Fugue. There will be no plot, no chronicle of events, no logic of discourse, but two themes, the Descent into Hades from

Homer, a Metamorphosis from Ovid, and, mixed with these, mediaeval or modern historical characters."[3] Pound later condemned Yeats' statement on the grounds that it had "done more to prevent people reading Cantos for what is *on the page* than any other one smoke screen."[4] The analogy to a "Bach Fugue" has indeed proven inadequate, if only to the sheer scope and inclusiveness of the poem, and once the hundredth canto had been written, with no end in sight, the limitations of Yeats' formula became obvious. Yeats' only error, of course, was to use such a tone of authority to report what could never have been more than tentative: the attempt of the poet, in 1928, to plan a poem that would be forty more years in the writing, and rooted in a life he had not yet lived, or even imagined.

Still, Yeats was only repeating what he had heard from Pound himself. Writing to his father in 1927, for example, Pound offered another version of his notion that *The Cantos* would assume a form analogous to that of a fugue, with a subject, a response, and a counter subject:

A.A.   Live man goes down into world of Dead
C.B.   The "repeat in history"
B.C.   The "magic moment" or moment of metamorphosis, bust thru from quotidien into "divine or permanent world." Gods, etc.[5]

From the perspective of 1944, on the other hand, he described the scheme of his poem in quite different terms: "For forty years I have schooled myself, not to write an economic history of the U.S. or any other country, but to write an epic poem which begins 'In the Dark Forest' crosses the Purgatory of human error, and ends in he light."[6] Elsewhere, he stoutly denied that his poem was an epic at all. Contradictions such as these have led critics to be very cautious about using Pound's own statements to define the form of his poem. Scattered as they are through letters and essays written over a period of many years, they may represent no more than passing moods or, at best, stages in a changing theory. But if they can be misleading about the overall form of *The Cantos,* they do offer very precise insights into how the poem functions in smaller details.

Pound filled his poem with figures out of a "divine or permanent world," and with men and women drawn from the very different world of human history. The initial problem for any reader of *The Cantos* is how so many people and events, scattered so widely in time and place, can ever be brought into meaningful order, in the absence of a narrative framework. One answer is contained in Pound's notion of the "repeat in history." Drawing on the very simple musical principle that a melody may be displaced in time (repeated later in the composition), or physically transformed, (played by different instruments) and yet remain identical in structure, Pound looked to the larger world of history and saw a similar possibility. Late in the twentieth century, in America, I may feel, or act, or even shape the whole pattern of my life in ways which are identical in structure with the act or the emotion of a man whose body has been dust for a thousand years. In the letter to his father, Pound called such resemblance a "subject-rhyme," and the concept became a useful shorthand for noting particular similarities, such as the reappearance of an idea: "Dante's view upon rectitude rimes certainly with that of Mencius." But it also underlies the most ambitious kinds of attempts to identify structures unifying great reaches of history: "From Kung to Mencius a century, and to St. Ambrose another six or so hundred years, and a thousand years to St. Antonino, and they are as parts of one pattern, as wood of a single tree."[7]

The concept of the subject-rhyme is a fundamental technique through which Pound was able to bring disparate details into relation in *The Cantos*. He came to it partly out of a need to invent some way of describing the significant patterns he saw in history, without resorting to the sort of generalization which only seemed to mask a writer's ignorance of particulars. Unlike generalization, which attempts to transcend any particular detail in order to arrive at a formula capable of accounting for many details, Pound's technique demands that particulars remain intact. As early as 1912 he had argued a doctrine of the "luminous detail," and thirty years later, in "A Visiting Card," his metaphor had not changed: "we need facts that illuminate like a flash of lightning." In *Guide to Kulchur*, Pound said that his aim as a writer was "revelation," and there is an obvious continuity between this later statement and his earlier efforts through the luminous detail, and then the image, to cause the reader to experience a sudden flash of insight. By the time he had begun writing *The Cantos*, however, Pound was interested in more complex insights than his imagist poems had attempted. He wanted to understand the interdependence of economics, politics, emotion, art, philosophy—and much more—in that cultural wholeness which is always in flux. He wanted to know why the ordered harmony of one age could sometimes be reborn amid the social disintegration of another.

If the revelation of the image was single and isolated, the next step was simply to seek to relate those isolated moments into meaningful patterns. Pound could begin to do so as soon as he learned to rhyme his details, to understand that two distinct realities might be linked in the mind, not through logic, but through a sudden act of perception. And from there it was only a little further to the fundamental technique of *The Cantos:* to select a great many concrete details and then to set them into relationship with each other in such a way that significant patterns might gradually be perceived. He called it the ideogrammic method, and he used it to construct individual passages, in which the juxtaposed details might be as brief as single words—as well as to construct the larger form of his poem, where images may fuse into pattern only over the space of hundreds of pages. Sometimes Pound's details seem private and puzzling, and his patterns fail to shine out. But when coherence does appear suddenly, out of so much matter, then his ideogrammic method achieves a poetry which is just as he imagined: "gristly and resilient," impossible to ignore.

II   *Visions of the Light*

The ideogrammic method was intended to convince the reader through its dependence on concrete detail rather than logical slither, and it was best suited for revealing complex order in what might appear to be a mere chaos of particulars. But since these ideogrammic patterns are seldom completed within the confines of a single canto, and since they are fundamental to Pound's vision in the poem, it is not possible simply to begin reading with the intention of understanding canto 1, and then move on to understand canto 2, and so on through the poem. Nor would I be any more successful in attempting to introduce the poem in that way. The most important structures within *The Cantos* are those threads which link recurrent images into larger patterns of insight, and my intention will be to throw light on the patterns themselves, even as they may occur over the span of many cantos.

Much of Pound's poem concerns the struggles of real men and women in history. But that world of human time, of individual acts and lives, is always framed by other visions: of an ordered beauty and justice brighter than anything we know on earth now; and of a contrary evil, a black hell of human malice. It is against those visionary extremes that Pound sets his moments of history, and posits the meaning of their endless struggle toward the light of justice, or the darkness of oppression. In some of his earliest poems, Pound had tried to depict moments of sudden visionary experience, brief glimpses of a reality other than that we know in our daily lives. In *The Cantos* he makes use of similar effects as, for example, at the beginning of canto 3, which opens in a kind of reverie as Pound remembers Venice, where he had come after losing his position at Wabash College. He had sat on the Dogana's steps and watched the city, and as the canto sets out a few very mundane details ("the gondolas cost too much, that year"), the shadowy reality of his own memory suddenly gives way before a reality totally other, a vision of mythic beauty:

> Gods float in the azure air,
> Bright gods and Tuscan, back before dew was shed.
> Light: and the first light, before ever dew was fallen.
> Panisks, and from the oak, dryas,
> And from the apple, maelid,
> Through all the wood, and the leaves are full of voices. . . .[8]

If the movement here is from reality to reverie to outright dream, it is also a movement of the imagination which is crucial to Pound's vision. Beyond the facade of a worn-out modern age, Pound has been able to see the vital forms which were there in the land all along, the gods whose animating power had been seed to the beauty of Florence or Venice.

In canto 4 Pound returns to his knowledge of the troubadours of medieval Provence to create a similar effect. He rhymes that world, partly historical at least, with images out of classical mythology: the myth of Philomela ("Ityn"—the child of Procne, cooked and served to his father) rhymes with the Provencal legend of the troubadour Cabestan, whose heart was served to

his lover by the latter's jealous husband; and then the figure of
Actaeon, devoured by his own hounds because he had looked on
the goddess Diana, naked, is set against Piere Vidal, the
troubadour who had dressed as a wolf and gone into the wilds for
love of his mistress, almost to die under the teeth of dogs. The
canto achieves an intricate interweaving of the two worlds, but
there is more to it than simply the demonstration of similarity in
tales such as these. Just as Pound had read about the
semifictional Vidal, Vidal has read, in Ovid's *Metamorphoses*,
about the entirely fictional Actaeon, and as he stumbles half
delirious through the woods, he thinks about the myth that
rhymes with his own reality. The movement is once again away
from reality toward legend, and then myth, and then dream, until
finally a purely visionary experience is attained:

> Thus the light rains, thus pours, *e lo soleills plovil*
> The liquid and rushing crystal
>   beneath the knees of the gods.
> Ply over ply, thin glitter of water;
> Brook film bearing white petals.
> The pine at Takasago
>   grows with the pine of Isé!
> The water whirls up the bright pale sand in the spring's mouth
> "Behold the tree of the Visages!"
> Forked branch-tips, flaming as if with lotus.
>   Ply over ply
> The shallow eddying fluid,
>   beneath the knees of the gods.

To Ovid's metamorphosis and its Provençal counterpart, Pound
now adds an Eastern image, two pines, at the Japanese seaport of
Takasago, which are said to contain the spirits of a husband and
wife. But Pound places the pines beside those of Isé, a Shinto
shrine to the sun goddess, and he focuses his image in the trees'
mutual growing. At the heart of that growing lies the goddess of
light itself, a "rushing crystal" which fills and animates and
unifies all things. As a kind of mystical union of fire and water it
flows up through the trees only to flame out at the branch tips,
and there to appear as lotus, the fire become a water lilly.

Pound's technique in this passage is characteristic of much of
The Cantos. If the reader can be expected to know the classical
tales of Philomela and Actaeon, he is less likely to be familiar
with that of Vidal, and very unlikely indeed to be able to

recognize the Japanese allusions. But the structure of *The Cantos* is such that we need not wait until every reference can be identified before we begin to read. Modern linguists speak of the principle of "redundancy" in language, referring to the fact that a sentence conveys the information necessary to make it grammatically meaningful in more than one way at the same time, thereby overcoming whatever "noise" may have interfered with its message for a hearer. There is an equivalent kind of redundancy in *The Cantos*. Pound's ideograms consist of details juxtaposed in such a way as to reveal some meaningful pattern. The particular details may be quite interchangable, and Pound does replace them with new ones as he repeats the ideogram (i.e., recreates the pattern) in successive cantos. Thus a reader might find that every time a particular ideogram appears some detail still remains obscure, and yet the unchanging structure which draws those details into relationship with each other may have become perfectly clear. Remembering Venice in canto 3, or placing the Middle Ages in conjunction with Greek myth, in canto 4, Pound has set down two concrete manifestations of a pattern which would otherwise only be available in a vague formula such as his "bust thru from quotidien into 'divine or permanent world.'"

This capacity to break through to a vision of the gods who flow like fiery water through every part of our world was important to Pound. In canto 2 he recounts the story of Dionysus who, traveling to Naxos, was kidnapped by sailors who fail to recognize him as a god. The penalty for their failure is harsh, as he changes them into fish. Only Acoetes escapes, because only he had been able to see beyond the surface of a familiar human form to the god within. The Dionysus who proceeds to reveal himself in that canto does so amid miraculously sprouting vines and the "heather smell of beasts," and for Pound the vision of the divine is always associated with the sort of organic wholeness which images such as wind, cloud, rain, tree, leaf, and beast suggest. The visionary "bust thru" of the early cantos offers the first access to a mythic world more fully explored later in the poem, as, for example, in canto 39, where the mortal Odysseus not only sees the goddess Circe, but unites with her. The context for their union is the cyclical renewal of the earth's fertility, and the canto is filled with images which emphasize the interconnections among all beings animated by the divine fire. Circe, however, is the goddess who turns men into swine, and who would make her union with Odysseus a permanent one. The seasons of her world are disordered ("late spring in the leafy autumn"), so that the vision in this canto moves beyond a mere discovery of the gods to an understanding that they move in the world according to an order of nature whose lines must not be overstepped.

In canto 47 that insight is represented in a more positive way. Odysseus is once again the central figure, as he frees himself from Circe to seek the advice of Tiresias in Hades, and ultimately to return to his human wife. Interwoven with the Odysseus motif are references to ancient Near Eastern rites celebrating the death and rebirth of Tamuz, a Babylonian fertility god associated with the cycle of the seasons. The god's death is symbolized by red lights drifting seaward, while at the altar wheat has been planted in shallow baskets to represent his rebirth. Reaching its emotional peak in the sorrowful lament of the people, the ritual was nevertheless designed to evoke a realization of the ordered harmony of nature. The god who dies is only a part of the larger pattern which includes us all, and Pound makes clear that beyond the vision of a god is the profounder vision that life goes on and must be lived according to its seasons. The task for mortal men and women is to coordinate their acts (e.g., spring plowing) with natural cycles which are revealed in such signs as cranes flying, or the Pleiades disappearing from the sky (*Cantos*, 237). Precise observation of nature is necessary to sustain this vision, and to carry it into action, but Pound also emphasizes the fact that the mystery at the heart of the vision, and of the ritual, is a sexual one. The blood of a mortal god is represented by light, his reborn body by sprouting wheat, and this mingling of symbolic categories (light, god, man, vegetable) is precisely the point. In sexual intercourse we may gain access to a crucial insight into our relationship with the rest of the living world:

> The light has entered the cave. Io! Io!
> The light has gone down into the cave,
> Splendour on splendour!
> By prong have I entered these hills:
> That the grass grow from my body,
> That I hear the roots speaking together,
> The air is new on my leaf,
> The forked boughs shake with the wind.

To the ancient Babylonians, Tamuz and the grain were sometimes interchangeable, symbolically. And for Pound that could be an image of metamorphosis in his own sense: a man and a tree are not equivalent, but if through some extraordinary event a man should become a tree, just for a moment, he would experience a revelation. The point is not to destroy the categories of being which distinguish man from tree, but only to bring them together long enough for a change of consciousness to take place, long enough for a man or woman to discover the intricate wholeness of the living world. That vision is seldom reached by Pound's characters, who labor through a history of isolation and narrow greed, but its possibility is always there, a part of everything that happens in the poem.

III   *Confucius*

In the mythology and the literature of classical Greece, Pound had found a vision against which he could measure the later course of European history. He had always been interested in finding the sources of inspiration which had led to periods of high civilization, and which might do so again, and in his 1914 essay called "The Renaissance," he announced a possible new source: "This century may find a new Greece in China."[9] Through the papers of Ernest Fenollosa, Pound had become interested in Chinese thought, and during the winter of 1914–1915, while he and and his wife were living in the country with W. B. Yeats, he began to read Confucius. Still involved with the notion that a new renaissance might be possible in his own time, Pound quickly saw China as a source of new thought analogous to the classical learning which had been rediscovered at the outset of our first, Italian, Renaissance. Although Greece remained important to him, he was coming to feel that its capacity to stimulate new creativity was almost worn out, and that in addition, the chance to establish genuine communication "with 400,000,000 living men, might seem to have certain advantages."[10]

In *Guide to Kulchur* (1938) he argued that "Confucius offers a way of life, an Anschauung or disposition toward nature and man and a system for dealing with both."[11] Distinguishing Confucian thought very carefully from philosophy, which has come to mean simply "a highbrow study, something cut off both from life and

from wisdom," Pound conceives of the Confucian system as
similar, and complementary, to those moments of visionary
metamorphosis in Greek mythology. Like the images of men who
mate with goddesses, or who find themselves changed into trees,
Confucian thought should lead to altered consciousness. It offers
an "anschauung"—literally a point of view, a way of seeing—and
its "disposition toward nature and man" is a stance toward the
totality of our experience, not merely a technique for analyzing
isolated problems. However, when Pound imagines gods over the
Italian lakes, or when Odysseus speaks with a goddess, the vision
can only be a temporary one—a glimpse beyond the limits of our
narrow human view and reaching, perhaps, to the very nature of
things—but temporary nonetheless. In Confucius, Pound saw a
vision which not only offered insight into nature and man, but
also offered a "system for dealing with both." Confucius could be
a way of bringing that brief, fragmentary vision of the myths
back down to earth, to seek in the conduct of our ordinary lives
an ordered harmony like that revealed in nature's larger world.

The Confucian concern with how human society ought to be
ordered appears most directly, and simply, in canto 13. In
dialogue with his followers, Kung (Confucius) speaks about
various ethical problems, but the focus of the canto is on his
fundamental assumptions. After several people speak about what
they would do if they were lord of a province, Kung is asked
which one had answered correctly, and he responds that "They
have all answered correctly, / That is to say, each in his nature."
The primary Confucian tenet behind that response was translated by Pound, in 1928, in this way: "The great learning . . .
takes root in clarifying the way wherein the intelligence
increases through the process of looking straight into one's own
heart and acting on the results; it is rooted in watching with
affection the way people grow."[12] The assumption here is that by
looking into our own hearts, we may see our true nature—and
that that nature is always good, unless it becomes lost and
distorted as we grow up into a society which is corrupt and
corrupting. In canto 13 Pound's formulation of this idea is
superficially similar to that of Wordsworth, as it affirms the value
of a child's natural innocence, particularly when contrasted to
the shameful spectacle of "a man of fifty who knows nothing."
Although both poets see the possibility that age may only lead to
greater ignorance, Pound views the child not as closer to some

glory prior to birth, but simply as closer to the nature of its own being, as not yet cut off from genuine self-knowledge by the artificialities of culture. Such knowledge is essential not only to personal fulfillment, but to the harmonious order of society. As Pound translates the Confucian vision in canto 13, all human order must begin with individuals—who are charged to set their own inner lives in order before all else. From that center in each human being, however, harmony can then be brought to families, and finally to the larger structures of society itself.

The conception is an organic one, and in Pound's rendering of Confucian thought, the pattern of one's own nature can be so significant not because it is a kind of arbitrary end-in-itself, but because it is continuous with the still more fundamental order of Nature, of which we are only one part. Thus it would be a gross distortion to take Kung's words to mean that we are free to impose our subjective whims on others. To look within the self, honestly, is *not* to find the selfishness of an isolated ego but, on the contrary, to find that we are connected with other human beings, and in fact with all living things in a pattern of vital relationship. In his translation of "The Unwobbling Pivot," Pound puts it this way: "getting to the bottom of the natures of men, one can thence understand the nature of material things, and this understanding of the nature of things can aid the transforming and nutritive powers of earth and heaven [ameliorate the quality of the grain, for example] and raise man up to be a sort of third partner with heaven and earth."[13] Translated into poetry, that Confucian vision of the wholeness of nature can be seen in canto 49, where rain, birds, men, and plants all seem to merge in a perfect harmony controlled by the changing seasons. If this canto serves as "the emotional still point of *The Cantos*," as Hugh Kenner described it,[14] it is also an image of how the perception of nature's order may be translated into the conduct of human lives:

> Sun up; work
> sundown; to rest
> dig well and drink of the water
> dig field; eat of the grain
> Imperial power is? and to us what is it?

Another critic of *The Cantos* has said that "in Pound's Paradiso,

East and West are joined,"[15] and that is precisely the insight
which ends this canto: "The fourth; the dimension of still-
ness. / And the power over wild beasts." Just as the Western
myths of Dionysius and Orpheus use the "power over wild
beasts" as a symbol for that state of awareness in which we break
through the apparent chaos of ordinary days and hours, and see
the changeless patterns of nature, so this Confucian vision of
organic harmony ends in the same image. So joined, the
profoundest insights of East and West provide one pole against
which human history can be measured in *The Cantos.*

IV *Hell*

Immediately following canto 13, where he first sets out the
harmonious Confucian ideal, Pound begins a series of cantos
which define his vision of the contrary extreme of blind, human
disharmony. It is between these two poles that Pound sees the
struggles of human history occurring. Written with Dante's
Inferno in mind, these cantos create a hell in which all the
categories of evil, as Pound saw it, are clearly revealed. Much of
cantos 14 and 15 are given over to violent invective which fixes
its sinners in a context of mud, stench, excrement, disease,
crawling insects, and vermin. The multiplicity of their sins,
however, can be reduced to one chief evil. If Pound's Good is the
power of vision which lets us see into nature and our own selves,
his Evil is precisely the opposite: the attempt to interfere with
that vision, to prevent or distort it. Whether it is denouncing
"bigots," Christian "vice-crusaders," "Panders to authority," or
scholars "obscuring the texts with philology," Pound's target is
essentially the same, because all of these figures may justly be
called "obstructors of knowledge." And that phrase is linked
with two other important categories: "monopolists" and
"obstructors of distribution." Pound condemns those who would
monopolize nature's goods, thus interfering with what should be
a continuous flow of those goods through a system composed of
men and women living in mutual dependence on one another,
and on the natural world which sustains them. In Confucian
thought, human beings must play a part in that process, actively
seeking to aid the "transforming and nutritive powers of earth
and heaven," and they must do so by learning to see as clearly as
possible into the nature of things. Thus any attempt to interfere

with our capacity to know the truth must result in a disruption of the proper harmony of man and nature. And conversely, any man who would seek a monopoly has failed to see beyond his own ego to the fundamental fact that he is vitally related to everything that lives.

Thus Pound's argument is essentially that modern Europe has become a hell of corrupt politicians and financiers, whose only concern is their own gain, and that such a condition exists because we can no longer see what the natural order of things ought to be. And that failure of vision is primarily the responsibility of "the betrayers of language," those journalists, statesmen, and professors who have been willing to pervert their language out of motives of personal greed, and disdain for the healthier "pleasures of the senses." Just as his imagist doctrines, and before that his imitations of late nineteenth-century symbolist verse had been in part a reaction against the misuse of language by those popular poets of the time whose work was sentimental, patriotic, and unfailingly rhetorical, so in *The Cantos* Pound continued to place great value on the proper use of language. If his early denunciation of bad style was mostly a question of taste, however, his assertion in canto 14 is more complex. Directing his rage against those few who oppress the many, Pound believes that they are able to succeed because they have so obscured language that the people can no longer see the light of truth. Such a fact is not simply unjust: it is a perversion of nature, and Pound emphasizes its consequences in images of "sadic mothers driving their daughters to bed with decrepitude, / sows eating their litters."

The point is that while Pound at one time may have valued precise language simply for artistic reasons, he gradually came to place greater emphasis on the social consequences of language and on its place in his increasingly comprehensive vision of things. Characteristically, the misuse of words in his hell is balanced elsewhere in *The Cantos* by numerous references to how language should ideally be used. The basic principle is Confucian, and in *Guide to Kulchur*, he translates it this way: "Tseu-Lou asked: If the Prince of Mei appointed you head of the government, to what would you first set your mind? KUNG: To call people and things by their names, that is by the correct denominations, to see that the terminology was exact."[16] This formula, which Pound repeats often, makes it very clear that precise language is central to good government, to the very order of society, not simply to good poetry. And set against the empty rhetoric of cynical politicians, which many other writers also rejected in the disillusionment following the end of World War I, Pound's Confucian tenet became one pole of a spectrum against which the health of particular historical eras might be measured. Complementing his transcendent vision of natural order with images of that order betrayed and perverted, Pound defines the outer limits of good and evil, within which ordinary life has always been lived. Essential to his definition of terms, hell is nevertheless not where the bulk of his poetry must lie, and at the end of canto 15 Pound emerges into the sunlight once again. In a letter to his father he called canto 16, which follows, a "purgatorio," but, more than that, its calmer, anecdotal treatment of World War I serves to lead the reader back into the world of human history, where the struggle must ultimately be played out.

CHAPTER 8

The Cantos: *Sailing Through History*

I   *The Voyage of Odysseus*

MANY of the cantos are concerned with history—particularly that of Europe during the Middle Ages and the Renaissance, of China from ancient times up to the eighteenth century, of the early years of the American republic, and of the modern Europe of Pound's own lifetime. Among the cantos devoted to history are passages which many readers find as difficult as anything in the poem, and the reason is obvious. These cantos seem to consist primarily of a staggering array of names, fragmentary anecdotes, quotations in several languages, and bits and pieces of suggestive imagery. Although that first impression is an accurate one, Pound's use of history is by no means opaque. In fact, it is really no more than an extension of poetic principles which have their roots in some of his earliest work. In his 1911-1912 series of essays, "I Gather the Limbs of Osiris," Pound had proposed his method of the "luminous detail" as an antidote to the modern weakness for either sentimentality, or biased generalization, or the uncritical heaping-up of every bit of evidence available. As a more effective way of leading people to insights they would *remember*, the luminous detail was a pedagogical device. But it was also an approach to history, in its suggestion that a few dozen carefully selected details can give us greater understanding of a period than any amount of long-winded generalizing.

As with so many of his early notions, Pound continued to refine this one, fitting it to the increasing complexity of his thought. In a sense he had already seen beyond imagism—with its intense, but

133

essentially isolated moments of perception—when he imagined that a cluster of details could stand for an historical period. He came to call that technique ideogrammic, and one of its chief uses in *The Cantos* was to try and see in history those patterns which draw the "facts" of a period into meaningful relationship. In an essay written in 1944 he spoke of history as *"an exposition of the nature of events,"* rather than simply an accumulation of facts.[1] If the patterns of relationship among a series of poetic details could be made congruent with the patterns which had actually related events at a moment in history, then Pound's readers would be able to grasp "the nature of events" directly, without the distortion and the distance of generalized narrative. Pound felt it necessary to invent such a technique because, for him, European philosophy since the Greeks had "degenerated into an attack on mythology and mythology is, perforce, totalitarian."[2] For Pound, mythology was a way of understanding reality without oversimplification, and without the sort of analysis which he saw as equivalent to the dissection of a living animal: knowledge bought at the cost of killing its subject. Looking to history, Pound saw the need to examine a reality that was organically whole, and to examine it in such a way as to grasp that unity, rather than destroy it. His poetic technique was a way of knowing equivalent to mythology in its capacity to preserve the concrete wholeness of its subject. And in Pound's eyes the most important aspect of any historical period was precisely its wholeness, its characteristic way of shaping the chaos of events.

In the work of the German anthropologist, Leo Frobenius, Pound found the term "Paideuma," which he defined as "the tangle or complex of the inrooted ideas of any period."[3] The concept was perfectly suited to Pound's own belief that culture is an orderly pattern in which each part is conditioned by the whole. When he discussed Paideuma his metaphors tended to be organic ("inrooted ideas"; "the gristly roots of ideas that are in action"), emphasizing that ideas are always the basis for social structure, and that those ideas are like seeds: just as seeds act to shape sun, water, and earth into living patterns, so ideas can draw the isolated acts of individual men and women into meaningful order. He spoke of Paideuma as "the active element in the era, the complex of ideas which is in a given time germinal, reaching into the next epoch, but conditioning actively all the thought and action of its own time."[4] It was precisely this complex of "germinal" ideas which Pound was concerned to reveal, through his ideogrammic method, in each of the historical periods which he treats in *The Cantos*.

As Pound actually began to shape his historical materials he was guided by a principle which further justified his ideogrammic method, though it complicated matters for his readers. In canto 13 he has Kung describe the proper treatment of history: though the practice seems to be disappearing, Kung can remember a time when historians would leave blanks in their writings, "for things they didn't know." Pound had already rejected historical generalizing for its inability to deal with the concrete wholeness of its subject, and in this Confucian principle he found yet another objection in the easy tendency of generalization to falsify, to simply cover ignorance with a smooth surface of prose. And this Eastern notion was complemented in his mind by a concept out of ancient Greece. In canto 47 Odysseus is instructed to go to Hades to see the dead prophet Tiresias. Though Tiresias is only a ghost, and his knowledge presumably even more insubstantial than he, still Odysseus must have it in order to complete his journey:

> Knowledge the shade of a shade,
> Yet must thou sail after knowledge
> Knowing less than drugged beasts.

The voyage of Odysseus was used by Pound as one of the structuring devices of his poem, just as Joyce used it for his *Ulysses*, though the parallel became less important as *The Cantos* developed over the course of many years. Pound's aim was to write a long poem that included history, and in that scheme Odysseus, exploring his Mediterranean space, was transformed into the figure of another kind of seeker, the poet whose journey is through the equally wide and dangerous sea of time.

Beside the *Odyssey*, Pound set another Greek work, *The Periplus of Hanno*, which described a voyage along the west coast of Africa. "Periplus" (circumnavigation) was a term which came to be used for any account of a coasting voyage, and Pound saw in it just the metaphor he needed to fuse his method—of building details into significant, ideogrammic clusters; and his aim—of seeking to know great reaches of history. He defined it in canto 59: "periplum, not as land looks on a map / but as sea bord seen by men sailing." Not the synthetic overview of the map's distant perspective, but the very different look of the coast itself, as men would see it from ships. The insight which Pound expressed in that image is central to a great deal of modern thought. R. Buckminster Fuller, for example, invented a Dymaxion world map which can be taken apart and assembled in many different ways, each time emphasizing the particular distortions of the observor's point of view.[5] While Marshall McLuhan's assertion that "the medium is the message"[6] really expresses the same insight: our knowledge of the world outside ourselves is conditioned in fundamental ways by the form our knowledge takes. To place Europe in the center of a map which relegates the "backward" continents to squeezed corners and edges is less an objective description of the world than it is a statement about our own point of view. Like Fuller and McLuhan, Pound was interested in finding new forms capable of expressing our knowledge of the world while still acknowledging what Werner Heisenberg, in still another discipline, would term the "uncertainty principle"—the impossibility, in nuclear physics as well as in poetry, of seeing a world that has not already been shaped by our methods of knowing.

Rejecting traditional ways of synthesizing history, Pound set out to sail through the past as Odysseus had sailed away from Troy, in periplum, confronting a coast that was always changing, always particular. Because he would map time instead of space, the rocks and beaches of the *Odyssey* became historical documents for Pound. But in taking them into his poem he adopted a technique which forced the reader to make the voyage with him, to confront history with the blanks left in. Bits of quoted documents, letters, anecdotes, dialogue, vividly imagined, but often fragmentary, scenes: these are the basic elements of Pound's treatment of history. In the last half of canto 40, he uses Hanno's *Periplus* directly, and the effect is, in miniature, like that of *The Cantos* as a whole. After a long sequence heavy with the details of struggling through a world of unfamiliar sights and sounds, strange men, wonderful discoveries, occasional beauty and much danger, the narrator concludes on a different note:

> Out of which things seeking an exit
> To the high air, to the stratosphere, to the imperial

      calm, to the empyrean, to the baily of the four towers
      the NOUS, the ineffable crystal. . . .

Pound sails through what seems at times an endless chaos of
history in *The Cantos*, but his sailing is sustained by visions like
this. This is the knowledge he sails for, and his goal is to find out
where, in the past, other men had found it, and let it shape their
lives.

II   *Sigismundo Malatesta*

Pound's journey through history begins with canto 1, which
translates a passage in the *Odyssey* in which Odysseus travels to
the underworld to speak with Tiresias. Like Odysseus, Pound
seeks knowledge, and he seeks it in the minds of men·long dead.
He cannot speak to them directly, as Odysseus does, but their
ghosts remain, nevertheless, if only in the words of old books.
Pound begins *The Cantos* with a concrete representation of the
way in which language contains the past. On one of his earliest
trips to Paris he had picked up a Renaissance translation of the
Odyssey, by Andreas Divus, published in 1538, and it is this
version that he himself translated in canto 1. However, in
translating it, he chose to use poetic conventions derived from
Old English verse. Pound knew that the shape of Odysseus's
quest has survived through millenia, but he also knew that the
means for its survival has been a long series of metamorphoses
into the particular words of new places, new times. If we would
seek ancient visions, we must seek them wherever they have
reappeared in the matter of successive cultures, and in canto 1
Pound reveals the complex filter of language and changing
culture which is nevertheless his only way of viewing the past.
    In succeeding cantos, Pound begins to move more fully into
history as he introduces a series of characters who range from
the highly fictionalized Cid, to the medieval troubadours,
Cabestan, Piere Vidal, Sordello, the Italian poets Arnaut Daniel
and Guido Cavalcanti, to the most colorful of medieval queens,
Eleanor of Aquitaine. However, the historical references of
cantos 2–7 tend to be rather brief and shifting, and they are
interspersed with a great deal of mythological material, as Pound
establishes the visionary axis of his poem. In passages like the one
in canto 4, where a mythic Actaeon is set beside the real Piere

Vidal, for example, Pound defines his belief that moments of history may share a common pattern, rhyming with each other and even with the ideal world of myth. It is not until cantos 8-11 that Pound begins his first extended excursion into a single historical period. His subject is Sigismundo Malatesta, a lord of Rimini during the fifteenth century, and Pound's chief example of a Renaissance soldier, schemer, lover, and patron of the arts. In many ways the Malatesta cantos are an ideal example of how Pound sets out to use history.

In accordance with his ideogrammic theories, Pound constructs his portrait of Sigismundo out of the very concrete matter which is all we really can touch of the past: letters, documents, facts out of old archives, anecdotes passed from book to book over the centuries. Beginning with a joking reference to T. S. Eliot, who had also used "fragments" to construct his *Waste Land*, Pound simply plunges his readers into the middle of Sigismundo's correspondence, without any of the traditional preparation of scene or character. Avoiding generalization, Pound gradually builds his picture of Renaissance Italy by amassing a great many specific details, and the effect for the uninitiated reader is something like walking into an archive to confront a series of unfamiliar names, allusions to events, letters dealing with situations apparently known only to the writer, and angry controversy in which it seems impossible to identify the antagonists or the issues. The antagonists and the events are there to be identified, of course, and scholars have already made it possible to find Pound's sources and explore the background of these cantos in some depth.[7] For many readers, however, the question remains whether scholarship of this sort is a necessary preliminary to reading the poem, or whether it simply increases the depth and complexity of our understanding. And for all Pound's fascination with obscure knowledge, Michael Reck probably comes closest to the mark when he says that "the poem means precisely what it says," that Pound presents things which he regards as significant in themselves, and that he is "intensely concerned with" the relations between those things.[8] Pound is not seeking to summarize any period of history, but rather to trace the lines of significant, recurring patterns which might be used to understand—and shape—the events of our own time. For Sigismundo's world, Pound has identified a pattern which is available on the face of his poem.

The character who emerges from canto 8 is, first of all, a man actively involved in the political struggles of his time, a soldier who knows how to conduct a war. Strong and resourceful, he deserves the tag which Pound grants him: polumetis—the Homeric epithet of Odysseus, meaning "of many devices." The link between these two heroes is intentional, of course, and it represents a basic rhyming of myth and history. Sigismundo is a hero who survives by his wit and courage in a world equally as dangerous as the one created by Homer. Surrounded by hostile, warring city-states, he serves one faction and then another as alliances shift and change. It is not as important to know why Florence and Venice were temporarily in league in 1449 as it is to know what the conditions of Sigismundo's life were like and how he dealt with them. In selecting very specific details to define how Sigismundo seems to have lived, in thought as well as action, Pound gives us a sense of the man, of the timeless, recurrent, Odyssean shape of his character. And further "background" information would only have directed the poem's focus away from that pattern and into the time-bound trap of history without vision.

Sigismundo's character, however, is not defined solely by his actions as a clever, courageous soldier. For Pound, Sigismundo's greatest achievement was his active patronage of the arts. Using his wealth and power as a ruler, Sigismundo had attempted to gather together the greatest artists of his time, among them Piero della Francesca, Leone Battista Alberti, and Agostino di Duccio. Their efforts were concentrated in building the Tempio Malatestiano, an impressive achievement in the style and spirit of the early Renaissance. As Pound reconstructs this aspect of Sigismundo's character, he appears as a man who is not only willing to spend his money in the service of art, but who has been concerned and sensitive enough to have learned something of the practical requirements of both art and artists. At the beginning of canto 8, for example, Pound translates a letter in which Sigismundo shows himself to be fully aware of technical problems (the walls cannot be painted because the mortar is still wet), and of the best emotional atmosphere for the creation and proper use of works of art (he will arrange for the artist to paint something else while the walls dry, "so that both he and I shall / Get as much enjoyment as possible from it"). But most important, he understands that art is just as much at the mercy of economic necessity as any other human activity, and so offers to guarantee Piero a lifetime income without any conditions attached. Pound was deeply resentful of the failure of modern governments to recognize that serious art is an essential part of any healthy society, and must therefore be granted its reasonable place in the nation's economy. That Sigismundo could do so, with such personal commitment, seemed to Pound to place him with those Confucian rulers whose vision of the properly ordered state was so much more inclusive, more natural, than the narrow concern for personal power and gain.

The portrait of Sigismundo which Pound creates out of the gradually assembled details of cantos 8 and 9 reaches its point of clearest focus in the series of letters which Sigismundo's enemies find upon intercepting his postbag. By dating the correspondence to 1454, the year in which the Malatesta fortunes began to fail, Pound establishes a background of dangerous political strife. But though Sigismundo might be expected to be concerned with nothing beyond his own survival at such a time, the letters reveal only the character of his household. In presenting a detail such as Sigismundo's gift of a pony to his six-year-old son, Pound defines a structure of relationships through the precise manipulation of tone. Thus, the young Malatesta thanks his father in language which expresses the respect and formality he was being taught through writing letters like this one, while still revealing a natural innocence and enthusiasm: the pony is "a fine caparison'd charger, upon which I intend to learn all there is to know about riding." Against the formality of the boy's letter, Pound sets a comment by his tutor, in a style which is sheer colloquial American: "It would take me a month to write you all the fun he gets out of that pony." The cumulative effect of these letters is to suggest the respect, decorum, affection, and businesslike free speaking which Sigismundo (as a true Confucian hero) has established as the heart of his properly ordered household.

In terms of content, however, these letters are mostly concerned with Sigismundo's patronage of the arts. Filled with the very concrete details of building—inventories of material, problems with securing proper measurements, waiting for the frosts to end before attempting to lay stone—they help to define a man whose overriding passion, even at a time when his political survival was threatened, was the creation of meaningful beauty. Canto 9 ends with a terse summary of the remaining contents of

the postbag, noting that Sigismundo "lived and ruled," and that
he had "built a temple so full of pagan works"

> and in the style "Past ruin'd Latium"
> The filigree hiding the gothic,
> > with a touch of rhetoric in the whole
> And the old sarcophagi,
> > such as lie, smothered in grass, by San Vitale.

San Vitale is a Byzantine church in Ravenna, nearly a thousand
years older than the Tempio, and by closing on this image of
time's inexorable passage, Pound imples that the vital new
achievements of Sigismundo's Reanissance must also fall before
the smothering grass of a world in constant flux. Sigismundo was,
for Pound, a man who had seen the vision, and who had struggled
to create a cultural vortex in his own time. But he was also a man
in history, and history was the destructive element in which
visions could be carried into action only in part, and only for a
time.

In cantos 10 and 11, Pound turns to the decline of Sigismundo's
power in the years after 1454. The surface of these cantos
appears equally as baffling as that of the first two, filled as it is
with unfamiliar names, fragmentary anecdotes, passages in
Italian and medieval Latin, and events pulled out of their
chronological context. Although a coherent history of fifteenth-
century Italy can be reconstructed easily enough, the complex,
fragmented, often opaque form of these cantos is essential to
their meaning, and ought to be respected. In its general outline,
Sigismundo's career was simple enough: ruler of a minor city, he
could survive only by exploting conflict among the greater
powers (Venice, Florence, Naples, the Vatican, etc.). When they
finally began to make more stable accommodations among
themselves, however, he found himself with too many enemies,
and few friends. Excommunicated by the pope, charged with
every crime from lechery to sacrilege, and burned in effigy on
the steps of St. Peter's in Rome, Sigismundo's power was finally
broken and he was left with Rimini and a few retainers. The point
of these cantos is not to tell Sigismundo's story, however, but to
make the nature of his world clear. And the pattern which
emerges is clear indeed: betraya murder, endless conspiracy,
alliances made and broken and made again, slander, vicious

competition, morality bought and sold. Such is the world of
history for Pound. And the effect of these cantos is, finally, to
reveal a bit of light in that darkness, to demonstrate that even in
a time as chaotic and violent as Sigismundo's, the vision of a
nobler order of society can be brought into action. When
Sigismundo is clearly bound for defeat, in canto 11, he sits in the
dark where an old woman nearly falls over him, and he thinks
about a peasant, who must be given "a decent price for his
horses." Flamboyant Renaissance tyrant though he might have
been, concern for the welfare of the people, for social justice,
was at the heart of his vision. Like the fires at the end of canto
11, lit by the common people to cheer him home, Sigismundo
shines in a dark time.

III   *China and America*

Through much of *The Cantos,* Pound is concerned with
history. Treating particular moments in the Middle Ages or the
Renaissance, in America before the Civil War, in Europe from
the Enlightenment down to the present, or surveying several
thousand years of Chinese history—and treating all this in
ideogrammic form—his poem has seemed impossibly difficult to
many readers. In the four Malatesta cantos, however, his most
basic assumptions about history are all present. For Pound,
history occurs somewhere in that space between the light of the
gods and the darkness of his hell of human oppression. The
divine harmony of nature is real, even though narrow human
concerns usually prevent our seeing it, and nothing was more
important to Pound than the need to attain the vision and then
translate it into action. History interested him whenever it
seemed to reveal that process, in the acts of a man like
Sigismundo, for example, who tried to make his love of mind, art,
and social justice manifest in the concrete reality of his own
state. Within the limited confines of the Malatesta cantos, Pound
is able to make the contrast between Sigismundo and his
disordered, oppressive age clear enough. And when he sets off
through larger tracts of history, in cantos which are not so
coherently focused on a single life, but move rapidly over details
drawn from many different times and places, his aim is still the
same: to find those moments when human beings have been

saved from the chaos and violence of time by the creation of a society which mirrors the harmony of nature.

Many critics have expressed some reservation about the cantos devoted primarily to history, particularly those dealing with Chinese history (52-61) and with John Adams (62-71). Noel Stock, for example, has pointed out a great deal of contradiction and needless obscurity in these cantos, and he argues that they represent a deterioration in Pound's use of language.[9] There is some justice in charges like these, though it could also be argued that Pound is simply recreating history with the blanks left in— with a vengeance. By not providing us with enough information about the names and events which fill his pages, Pound makes it very difficult to understand the content of many of these cantos. However, meaning does not reside in "content" alone, and the attempt to trace his sources and then reconstruct his subject matter in a fully coherent way may simply be "wrong from the start." Pound's poem is primarily concerned to reveal essential patterns within history, and the full "story" of any individual detail is far less important than its function in relation to other details. While we may often be unsure about what aspect of an historical event Pound may have been alluding to through mention of a name or a date, we are seldom in doubt about what *value* he attaches to the detail. His details are clearly "marked" in this regard, and when he combines them into clusters and then reproduces those clusters over and over again—their structures remaining the same while the details which constitute them change—the larger patterns of history as Pound sees it gradually become clear.

Pound sets Sigismundo Malatesta near the beginning of his poem as a paradigm for his approach to history and a first example of the sort of hero he most admired. But that portrait is balanced by the far more elaborate treatment of China and John Adams, which concludes this phase of *The Cantos*. In surveying nearly four thousand years of Chinese history, Pound proceeds according to a few simple principles which organize what would otherwise be a bewildering array of unfamiliar names. He begins, in canto 52, by establishing the Confucian vision of natural harmony as recorded in the *Li Ki*, or *Book of Rites*. After briefly recalling the decadence of Western culture, the canto turns to Confucian wisdom as a clear alternative. As Pound presents it, that wisdom consists essentially of precise observation of the seasons and the natural cycles of all living things, accompanied by rules for human conduct which act to place men and women firmly into that world of nature:

> Now mares go to grazing,
>   tie up the stallions
> Post up the horsebreeding notices
>   Month of the longest days
> Life and death are now equal
>   Strife is between light and darkness
> Wise man stays in his house
>   Stag droppeth antlers
> Grasshopper is loud,
>   leave no fire open to southward.

Proceeding through the seasons to create a picture of human activity in perfect balance with natural process, the canto concludes by stating some basic Confucian principles ("Call things by the names. Good sovereign by distribution / Evil king is known by his imposts"), and then pointing to the Western example of Lord Palmerston as a just, practical head of state.

Having established the fundamental Confucian vision in canto 52, Pound turns back to the time of the earliest emperors, who are remembered as the almost godlike originators of culture. From that beginning, Pound moves down through nearly two thousand years to the time of Confucius himself, and then on into a history whose principles are really very simple. While emperor succeeds emperor and dynasties rise and wane, the order of society depends on how closely the Confucian ideals are being followed at any point in time. When society is governed by Taoists, Buddhists, or ambitious court eunuchs, then suffering and disorder is the lot of the people. The impression conveyed by much of these cantos is that history is an endless struggle for wealth and power, fought out among men who care little for the welfare of the people, and who know nothing about the roots of their own actions. Set against that chaos, however, is the recurring success of rulers who understand the Confucian vision, and put its principles into action. For Pound, the Confucian ideal was a pattern, rooted in the process of nature itself, and always available to shape the constantly changing matter of history: every day to "make it new." If time's endless movement destroys the order of our world, then that order must be endlessly recreated by men and women able to shape new events to the lines of an old pattern.

Throughout the Chinese cantos, Pound structures his vast array of detail by means of the simple set of juxtapositions, Confucian / non-Confucian, ordered / disordered, and natural / unnatural. Thus in canto 54, for example, Pound associates the name of a poor ruler with images of nature disordered ("Rain of blood fell in Y-yang/pear trees fruited in winter"), while a good emperor is defined by actions which make it possible for all people to live by nature's bounty (e.g., reducing taxes, assuring that farmers are provided with the necessary tools). Tracing his pattern through countless particulars, Pound finally ends, in canto 61, with the eighteenth century, where he finds the teachings of Kung still alive in the works of the emperors Yong Tching and Kien Long. From a plan to relieve the people in time of famine, to tax incentives for the cultivation of new land, to a free dinner for the most honest citizens of each town ("no favour to men over women"), a regime like Yong's represents the basic Confucian ideal that "a good governor is as wind over grass," that a ruler's primary concern must be for the good of the whole people, and that he must understand precisely how they are dependent on him, on each other, and on the earth which sustains them all.

The Chinese cantos begin with images out of Western history, and near the end of canto 61 they return to the West with a brief reference to the rise of the Adams family in America during the years when Yong Tching ruled China. The conjunction of East and West was, of course, very important to Pound, and at this point in the cantos he is able to justify it in two ways. Cantos 59 and 60 deal with the first modern contacts between China and Europe, and at the end of canto 60 Pound asserts what is for him a crucial link, in the eighteenth-century French Jesuits whose mission to China had put the European Enlightenment in touch with ancient Confucian thought. Just as the foundation of the Académie française in 1635, charged with maintaining the purity of the French language, had seemed essential to the establishment of a rationally ordered civilization, so in China Kung had taught that to "call things by their right names" was indispensable to the preservation of any just society. For Pound, it was no incidental similarity, but a cultural rhyme of great significance, and when he sets the French injunction ("et qu'on n'employât que des termes propres") beside its Chinese counterpart ("CH'ing ming"), he emphasizes that however distant two cultures may be in space or language, they may be shaped, at some level, by identical patterns of thought.

Beyond the mutual influence of Chinese sage and traveling Jesuit, it was this notion of rhymes in history which provided Pound with his second link between the China of Kung and the America of John Adams and Thomas Jefferson. Just as China had continued to produce wise, Confucian emperors through centuries when chaos and misrule always threatened, so in the early years of the American republic men appeared who could be rhymed with the greatest leaders of other eras. Cantos 62-71 are devoted to John Adams, one such Poundian hero. But while the series of Chinese cantos is rather self-contained (cantos 13 and 49 are the notable exceptions), Pound prefigures the Adams series in a good many of his earlier cantos. In part, the reason lies in the fact that figures such as Adams and Jefferson do not simply stand as models in Pound's gallery of the past. Like Sigismundo, or the great emperors of China, they represent yet another incarnation of a timeless pattern, but they also stand at the beginning of our own historical era. Thus Pound introduces Jefferson at the beginning of canto 31 by quoting the motto of the Malatesta family: "Tempus loquendi / Tempus tacendi" (there is a time to speak, there is a time to be silent), and thereby announces a link between these two men. But then as he proceeds to construct the ideogrammic cluster of detail which will define the lives of Jefferson and Adams, Pound moves quickly on into the nineteenth century, weaving in material from the presidencies of J. Q. Adams, Jackson, and Van Buren. Turning to Europe he introduces the Napoleonic wars, Karl Marx, the various industrial reform movements of mid-century, and then Mitteleuropa: where World War I was spawned, and the modern world began to be.

For all his long study of the past, it was really his own age that interested Pound most. But what he saw all around him was a society firmly under the control of the bankers, the corrupt politicians, the munitions makers—men like Metevsky, in canto 38, who sells his guns to both sides, always encouraging the mutual fear and distrust which makes him rich. It was into that world of selfish oppression that Pound wanted to introduce the values which, in the America of Jefferson and Adams, had once promised to redeem a dying civilization and which might be made to do so yet. The cantos which deal with the history of Europe and America from the eighteenth century to the present are filled with as much difficult, even obscure material as anything Pound has written, and for many readers the Adams sequence has seemed especially arid as poetry. As I have argued earlier, however, Pound is primarily interested in reshaping the future, and therefore he would seek not the *substance* of the past—which can never recur—but its *pattern*—which can shape the substance of new lives endlessly. In exploring the period which he termed "American civilisation, 1760 to 1830," Pound was seeking "the possibilities of revival, starting perhaps with a valorisation of our cultural heritage."[10]

To Pound, "civilisation" meant a system of social organization which valued more than the "mere acquisition of profit." The pattern which gradually emerges out of the reiteration of many cantos shows the ideal leader to be a person who values art as well as politics. Thomas Jefferson, for example, in canto 21, writes to Burgundy in the hope of finding a gardener who can also play the French horn, and so complete his economical chamber orchestra. And in canto 34, John Quincy Adams, while president, reveals an interest in the precise observation of nature:

> They (congress) wd. do nothing for
> the education of boys but to make soldiers, they
> wd. not endow a university (in 1826).
> Black walnut, almond planted in spring
> take two months precisely to vegetate to the surface.

Pound deliberately sets Adams´s interest in nature beside his conduct of government (and underlines the pattern by repeating it two more times), because the two are intimately related. Just as Confucius had taught that the Great Learning "is rooted in watching with affection the way people grow," so Adams knew that good government must be rooted in the same natural process which rules all living things. Growing boys, like growing trees, must receive careful nurture, and society ought to recognize their fullest human potential, not merely their narrow capacity to become soldiers.

Perhaps the most important to a fully human society, in Pound's eyes, was economic justice. The theme is often sounded in pithy injunctions: " 'Thou shalt not,' said Martin Van Buren, 'jail 'em for debt' "(canto 37). Or, a page later, " 'No where so well deposited as in the pants of the people, / Wealth ain't,' said President Jackson." This canto, which deals with the efforts of Van Buren to curb the increasingly powerful banking system, is one climax in Pound's treatment of the attempt by private interests to gain control of the public wealth, through the creation of a centralized federal bank and a national debt. Though men like Jackson and Van Buren tried to stop them, the bankers ultimately prevailed, preparing the way for the economic oppression which is Pound's chief subject when he treats his own age in *The Cantos*. The kinds of oppression which Pound notes range from the outright ownership of human beings, condemned by Jefferson in a "vehement philippic against negro slavery" (376), to such qualified forms of enslavement as arbitrarily excluding women from power (411), or creating debts which future generations must pay. If Pound had set out to explore the past in search of patterns more just than those he saw in his own time, he found in the American past a special case. Convinced that American culture might yet be shaped to the best of history's patterns, Pound saw that best embodied, during the early days of the Republic, in the lives of men like Jefferson and Adams. Insofar as *The Cantos* are a journey through history, their purpose is to make those patterns out of the past available to the present, and the future.

CHAPTER 9

Deeper Harmonies

I *Economics*

IN the fall of 1924 the Pounds left Paris and moved to Rapallo, a small town on the Italian Riviera. Tired of what had begun to seem a decadent, worn-out world of letters in Paris, Pound looked to Italy for an imaginative richness like that he had gathered in his recently published Malatesta cantos. Though Pound was apparently little interested in modern Italian politics at the time, Mussolini had come to power in 1922, and he too gradually became a part of Pound's vision. To Pound he appeared to be an active leader who saw the importance of art in his plans for the general welfare of the people, and by 1935 Pound could write a book entitled *Jefferson and/or Mussolini*. Many writers began to involve themselves with politics during the thirties, of course, but to some extent Pound had always been interested in such questions. If his early dreams of a new American Renaissance had emphasized changes that were mostly cultural, he gradually came to see that the artistic and intellectual life of a nation rests to a considerable extent on an economic foundation. In 1918 he had met Major C. H. Douglas, whose Social Credit movement would help to focus his sense of economic injustice and provide him with what seemed entirely reasonable solutions. Armed with new theories, and feeling the excitement of change in Italy, Pound began to move beyond the spirit of waste and despair which had been so pervasive at the close of World War I. In Rapallo he devoted more and more of his energy—and his poetry—to the suddenly hopeful task of building the world new once more.

For many of his readers, Pound's increasing involvement with

politics and economics was entirely a mistake, a strange
aberration which led him to waste his lyrical gifts on unsuitable
subjects, and eventually to stand accused as a traitor to his
country. For those who take this view, there has often seemed to
be a failure of coherence in Pound's thought. This man obsessed
with banks and credit seems to bear no relation to the poet who
could evoke so beautifully the lost splendor of Venice, gods in
the clouds above Sirmio, or nature's intricate process. There is
greater coherence in Pound's thought, however, than might at
first seem apparent. One of the clearest focal points for the
economic concerns of *The Cantos* is canto 45, a kind of litany
against the practice of usury. One critic has called this canto a
"repudiation of complex issues," charging that Pound over-
simplifies "a problem as complicated as the relationship of art,
life, and society."[1] The poetic surface of the canto is indeed
simple. But simplicity of statement does not imply simplicity of
vision, and in this canto Pound is asserting that society must be
understood whole, that it is in fact an enormously complex unity
composed of countless interrelated elements. Pound brings
together a wide range of the elements that make up a society—
from wheat and baked bread to painting, sculpture, architecture,
the crafts of sewing and weaving, and even the sexual union of
bride and bridegroom—and he ascribes their degeneration in
modern times to the abuses of usury. If this seems to be no more
than a misuse of the principle of cause and effect, the truth is
more complicated. In attempting to describe the wholeness of a
culture, Pound begins with the assumption that society is not a
collection of unrelated things, but a fabric of relationships in
which a change in any one part is felt throughout the whole
system.[2] To study these relationships, however, is not simply to
catalog all the elements of a system, but to examine the way in
which those elements intersect. The principle is clear in this
canto: "with usura the line grows thick/with usura is no clear
demarcation." Just as Confucius had taught that the first step
toward harmony in human society is to call things by their right
names, so Pound understood that discrimination is simply the
twin of relation, that the same line which connects two points
also separates them. He was interested in social pattern, and to
him the most fundamental lines of connection in any society
could be seen through economics.

The choice, though disturbing to the poetic expectations of

many readers, is a good one if Pound's understanding of the subject is taken seriously. Although money may be thought to have value in abstraction—that is, thought of as *thing*—it is really only the visible sign of a system of relationships in which "the abundance of nature,/with the whole folk behind it" (257), constitutes the matter. The function of money is, simply, to facilitate the distribution of that abundance among the members of a society. In this sense it has no reality of its own, but operates instead to place the elements—wheat, bread, weavers, painters, builders—in such a relationship to each other that a viable pattern, i.e., a society, can come into being. The "obstructors of distribution" in Pound's hell are there because they have blocked the flow of money which must be continuous if the pattern is to be maintained. For Pound society is not a static pattern like bricks in a wall, but a dynamic (and therefore unstable) pattern more like planets in a solar system or steel chips in a magnetic field. If the flow of force is interrupted, the system will begin to come apart. So with usury, an extra charge is added to the cost of production which cannot be recovered by the workers when the objects produced are sold—and thus their buying power will always be less than the cost of the available goods. Or put another way, some of the money which must continue to circulate to keep the system in balanced relationship will leak away to the bankers. And when the field of force changes, the objects in it may be distorted: if bread no longer comes naturally to the painter, because money is piling up somewhere else in a blocked system, then his art alters in compensation: "no picture is made to endure nor to live with/but it is made to sell and sell quickly. . . ." Canto 45 is Pound's most concise description of the central importance of economics to the just, orderly society he sought.

II   The Pisan Cantos

Throughout the thirties, Pound's interest in economic reform grew, and he promoted his schemes in countless letters, pamphlets, conversations, and articles published in magazines which spanned the political spectrum from Italian Fascist publications to the Communist *New Masses*. Though he had lived in Europe for many years, he still followed developments in America closely, always hoping to convince anyone who would listen that the principles of men like Jefferson and Adams might still be invoked to redeem a degenerate age. In 1939 he even returned to the United States to speak directly with a number of congressmen, senators, and other officials, such as Henry A. Wallace, then secretary of agriculture. Though he found a few sympathetic listeners, recorded some poems, and received an honorary degree from his old college, his trip was a failure, and after two months he sailed back to Genoa. Europe was on the verge of war, and when it came several months later, the remainder of Pound's life received its shape. In 1941, still hopeful that he could convince his countrymen of their folly in ignoring his ideas, he began to broadcast over Rome Radio. After Pearl Harbor, he reportedly tried to board the last train carrying Americans out of Italy, only to be turned away by the U.S. chargé d'affaires. By the summer of 1943 he had been indicted for treason, and two years later he sat in a cage at Pisa, in a camp designed to hold the American army's most dangerous criminals. Ahead lay bitter controversy and a trial which ended with a verdict of insanity, and twelve years of confinement at St. Elizabeth's Hospital, in Washington, D.C.

While he was a prisoner at Pisa, Pound wrote a new series of cantos which were at once a powerful expression of his personal tragedy and a renewed assertion of all he had valued in life as well as poetry. As might be expected, *The Pisan Cantos* are partly concerned with the past, and the sense of loss is strong. Drawing details from his personal memories of men like Ford Maddox Ford, W. B. Yeats, and James Joyce, who had been with him at the beginning of the struggle to establish the modernist movement in literature, Pound builds these cantos out of a past more immediate than Sigismundo's Renaissance or the China of Confucius. From the briefest allusion, to extended anecdotes like that in canto 83 (where Pound recalls Yeats composing poetry during the winter they spent together at Stone Cottage in Sussex, in 1914) *The Pisan Cantos* represent Pound's attempt to find, in his own life, the "luminous details" which had shaped his past and which might still redeem the crushing failure of his present.

As an attempt to gain greater self-knowledge, these cantos move through a variety of moods, from despair, to self-justification, to confession: "J'ai eu pitié des autres/probablement pas assez, and at moments that suited my own convenience" (460). Just as Pound had always condemned injustice in highly

moral tones that betrayed his roots in puritan America, so in
adversity he feared that his own suffering must somehow be
deserved, that he had perhaps failed to feel sufficient pity for
the hardship of others. Elsewhere, Pound presents himself as
essentially innocent, though weary and defeated: "Old Ez folded
his blankets/Neither Eos nor Hesperus has suffered wrong at my
hands" (488). Through all his self-questioning, however, as he
contemplates the meager details of a prison camp, or dreamlike
scenes out of memory, Pound struggles to understand how
anything of value can endure in the midst of so much change. In
the earlier cantos, he had explored the chaos of history in search
of insight capable of redeeming his own degenerate age, and
what he found was simply pattern. Intangible, existing only
through the temporary lives of men and women, pattern was
nevertheless the only enduring thing in our time-ravaged world.
In *The Pisan Cantos,* Pound explores the far more limited history
of his own life, and what he finds there is change as complete,
and as terrifying, as any shift in the fortunes of a medieval town
or a modern nation. And here too, all that endures is a pattern
that no one can touch:

> nothing matters but the quality
> of the affection—
> in the end—that has carved the trace in the mind
> dove sta memoria. . . .
>
>   (457)

If memory is almost all Pound has to work with in *The Pisan
Cantos,* the process by which he reaches back to "where one
remembers" is essentially a stripping away of all the physical
substance of his life, a loss of his personal history. In canto 80, he
notes that if he must leave Italy he will bring with him only "one
Eucalyptus pip" which he had picked up on the road out of
Rapallo, as he was being led away into captivity. Earlier, he had
referred to "Eucalyptus that is for memory" (435), and the single
pip is an ideal image of Pound's vision in these cantos. For the
poet, who can pick it up and put it in his pocket, it is a very
tangible sign of how little is left him of sixty years of life. And yet
it is also a seed which bears within it the living pattern of another
tree. For Pound, memory is like that: almost nothing itself, but
still a way of starting over, a seed. Of course, it is not simply a

question of remembering the transitory details of one's life. As Pound uses it in *The Pisan Cantos*, memory must involve an insight which transcends the time-bound surface of things. Like the luminous details of his early poetry, or the clustered bits of document in the history cantos, these images out of his own past must renew Pound's access to the timeless patterns which sustain the world.

Pound establishes his basic theme, in canto 74, as a movement from destructive chaos, which leaves him without identity, to the rediscovery of a vision more real than any merely human identity has ever been. Returning to the motif of Odysseus which had begun *The Cantos*, he sees himself as OΎ TIΣ, No-man—a name which Odysseus had used to trick the Cyclops, but which in 1945 named Pound's own condition:

OΎ TIΣ
a man on whom the sun has gone down
nor shall diamond die in the avalanche
            be it torn from its setting
first must destroy himself ere others destroy him.

Like Odysseus, Pound would save himself by seeming to destroy himself. However, Pound's endeavor is no trick, but rather a painful attempt to unravel the fabric of his life and so find the few essential threads. If history is the avalanche which threatens to destroy him, there is nevertheless a diamond which no change can touch, and Pound makes its nature clear in the continuation of this passage, where he alludes to an African folktale. "Gassire's Lute" recounts the struggles of men to attain a divine city which appears on earth four times, only to be lost each time through some human vice. But the city will appear once again, this time as an ideal, spiritual pattern, and in that form it will remain forever, indestructible. To Pound, who had watched his own version of the holy city take shape among documents of the past, only to be swept away in time's flowing, again and again, Gassire's city of the mind was his indestructible diamond. Personal salvation in despair, pattern for the future as well as the past, it was what the seed in his pocket meant.

As Pound weaves this motif into *The Cantos*, he carefully associates it with similar images. At the beginning of canto 74, for example, he asserts his dream in the face of much ruin: "To build the city of Dioce whose terraces are the colour of stars." Linking this image of Ecbatana, ancient capital of the Medes, with a miraculous city out of African legend, Pound later associates it with Mt. Segur (510), the site of a castle in Provence, besieged during the Albigensian Crusade, which was responsible for the destruction of the Provençal culture which Pound so much admired. Thus on the one hand these allusions all point to worthy dreams which could not be made to endure amid the folly and the violence of the world of time: "and in Mt. Segur there is wind space and rain space" (452). And yet they are also open to the question which Pound asks a page later, with reference to the lost justice of Hebraic law: "Why not rebuild it?" Of course, Pound had always understood the destructive power of history — in canto 23, for instance, he placed Mt. Segur and the ruins of Provençal civilization beside the fallen city of Troy. *The Pisan Cantos* add a dimension of personal urgency to that picture of old forms destroyed, but their central endeavor is still to recover the vision, and build anew.

From his earliest lyrics, there had always been an element of the visionary in Pound's verse, and in *The Pisan Cantos* that element is strongly present again, as a way back to life for the poet and his ruined Europe alike. In canto 74 he affirms his will to continue the struggle in terms which emphasize the intermingling of politics and vision. There is a kind of equivalence for Pound between terms as different as the constitution, a legendary city, and the goddess Aphrodite appearing before Anchises, the mortal man she would take as lover. For Pound the vision of a goddess, the memory of past greatness, and the legal charter for a government may all act as seeds to structure the stuff of history. Each offers access to the patterns which, like wind and rain, are vital to life, and which, finally, are rooted in the process of nature itself.

To some extent, Pound has always been a poet of nature, and in *The Pisan Cantos* nature assumes a central place in his thought. From clouds over the mountains, to birds on the telephone wires to the dwarf morning glories near his tent, Pound continually uses nature as the vehicle of his perception. The process can be seen as fully, and as beautifully, as anywhere in the passage in canto 83 where he watches the birth of a wasp. He begins by observing how the wasp had built its mud house, and how the infant had first "stuck its head or tip" out, and then moves to the emotional rest which this communion offers: "When the mind swings by a grass-blade,/an ant's forefoot shall save you." The infant wasp, almost indistinguishable from the grass blades, goes down into the chthonic realm of earth (XTHONOS), and in his going he becomes identified with the Odysseus who had begun that journey in the very first canto. The purpose of his going is to establish communication with that other world ("to carry our news," to "have speech with Tiresias") and in doing so he appears to become part of it ("like to like colour"). Odysseus / Pound begins his journey to Hades in canto 1 in order to find out the way home, but by *The Pisan Cantos* he has learned that, in one sense, Hades is XTHONOS, and XTHONOS is earth, and earth *is* his home. In canto 77, Pound writes that "the forms of men arose out of γέα" (earth), while in canto 82 he offers what is perhaps his most succinct statement of this insight: "man, earth: two halves of the tally."

Many years before, in "Psychology and Troubadours," Pound had written of our "kinship to the vital universe, to the tree and the living rock." He spoke of certain minds which he called "germinal": "Their thoughts are in them as the thought of the tree is in the seed, or in the grass, or the grain, or the blossom. And these minds are the more poetic, and they affect mind about them, and transmute it as the seed the earth. And this latter sort of mind is close on the vital universe."[3] Even then he had conceived of mind as seed, and of a tree as structured by thought. In *The Pisan Cantos* he returns to the explicit statement of this kinship between man and nature:

> The ant's a centaur in his dragon world.
> Pull down thy vanity, it is not man
> Made courage, or made order, or made grace,
>   Pull down thy vanity, I say pull down.
> Learn of the green world what can be thy place
> In scaled invention or true artistry,
> Pull down thy vanity,
>   Paquin pull down!
> The green casque has outdone your elegance.

In these lines Pound concludes his turning away from one of the most fundamental attitudes of hundreds of years of European culture. He rejected that belief which, in thought, culminated in the nineteenth century's optimistic faith in scientific progress, and which, in physical consequence, has not yet finished: that man is a being set apart from nature, that in the power of a reason which knows no natural limits, man will master the earth and shape it to his own desires. But Pound/Odysseus is of Gea, earth, and these lines are the affirmation of that identity. That man might reenter the natural world, and thereby alter his perception irrevocably had occurred to Pound as early as "The Tree," and the figure of human beings transformed into beast or plant recurs throughout his poetry. In *The Pisan Cantos* Pound confronted the individuality of his own life, recalling friends and places and ideas which all seemed to have perished. One consequence of that reverie was to emphasize how fleeting and insubstantial are the acts of any individual, unless those acts are rooted in patterns more permanent than the superficial shape of a few decades of human history. Pound's need in these cantos was to redeem the wreckage of events by finding his way back to the ground of his being. As Confucius had taught, and as Pound himself had known very early, that ground is Nature itself. Whatever peace these cantos find is rooted in Pound's full, explicit acknowledgment that his own power of knowing depends absolutely on the earth which he has been forced to see close-up once more, as he lies on the ground and smells the mint leaves growing beside his tent.

III   *The Later Cantos*

During the years he spent at St. Elizabeth's Hospital in Washington, Pound continued to work on *The Cantos*, and to a large extent he continued to be what Gertrude Stein had disapprovingly called him—the "village explainer,"[4] intent on saving the world through the resurrection of lost causes. But the painful self-awareness of *The Pisan Cantos* was not forgotten. Though some critics have refused to credit Pound with any capacity for insight into his own actions,[5] he was in fact deeply concerned with knowing—and judging—himself. In his last years he fell into a silence that seemed to cover a sense of guilt and failure. Speaking to Allen Ginsberg, in 1967, he confessed that "the worst mistake I made was that stupid, suburban prejudice of anti-Semitism."[6] And at the end of *The Cantos* he tried to see his work whole:

> But the beauty is not the madness
> Tho' my errors and wrecks lie about me.
> And I am not a demigod,
> I cannot make it cohere.

A few lines later he qualifies feeling with understanding:

> to "see again,"
> the verb is "see," not "walk on"
> i.e. it coheres all right
>   even if my notes do not cohere.

No word he could have chosen would have been as precisely right as "cohere" to focus the central concern of *The Cantos*—or to name its relevance to twentieth-century thought. One of the agencies for radical change in our time has been an altered perception of how the world coheres—whether we are considering the structure of society, the relationship of individual men and women, or the patterns within atoms. We are obsessed with how the world goes together because it has come apart in our minds. The old order has fallen away in countless limited details every day of our experience, and something else has begun to replace it. Pound had lived the change. He had been led out of the nineteenth century gradually, and in *The Cantos* he had tried to create a poetic form which would force the reader to seek a new order. For Pound, the old generalizations had made us blind to the interdependence of all things, had made it possible for the rich man to imagine he had no relation to the poor man he exploited, and for all of us to imagine that we had somehow got free of earth's natural process.

On the last page of *The Cantos* Pound speaks of his failure in trying to create an earthly paradise: "That I lost my center/ fighting the world." But if Pound's poem, like his life, does contain mistakes, and too much anger, it also contains as clear a view of what our center must be as any major work of its time. Like the emperor in canto 99, who "watched things grow with affection," Pound came to know that human truth is always rooted in the larger truth of nature. Speaking about the need to find a language of poetry which renders the world as precisely as possible, Ernest Fenollosa had written that "all processes in nature are interrelated,"[7] and that statement could serve as text for the form as well as the content of *The Cantos*. To learn to see pattern in the apparent chaos of history was the task Pound set himself, and by the late cantos he had moved beyond the specific patterns of ancient China and new America to a fascination with the nature of structure itself, with "Catholicity,/Woven in order" (695). Seeking wholeness in a world shattered by economic and political crisis, Pound saw the need to shift his perception away from individual events and toward the fabric of relationship which unites them. In canto 103 he turns this principle into a yardstick for judging the relative value of different ways of perceiving, attributing the greatest success to the ancient Chinese emperor, Yu: "I see its relation to one thing,/Yu sees its relation to ten."

In valuing such perception, and in creating a poetic form which forces us to seek out complex patterns of relationship within material which spans hundreds of pages of verse, Pound was exploring a mode of thought which has become central to much of the intellectual advancement of the twentieth century. For example, Gregory Bateson, the anthropologist, has discussed the possibility of seeing an analogy between the formal pattern which relates stem, leaf, and bud in a flowering plant, and that which relates "different sorts of words in a sentence."[8] And in fact, in linguistics, communication theory, anthropology, design, painting and sculpture, and ecology much of the significant innovation of recent years has come from just the sort of approach which Bateson describes. The extent to which a shift of method such as this constitutes a reorientation in how we perceive the order of the world, and our place in that order, should not be underestimated. When Einstein posited that matter might be transformed into energy, the transformation he described was already underway in the European mind: the nineteenth century's solid fruit had become planes of relation in Braque and Picasso; Freud transformed personality from stable essence into a configuration of dynamic forces set in motion by the events of personal history; anthropologists like Malinowski, Mead, and Benedict began to search out the rules of relationship through which particular societies united their individual members.

For his own springboard, Pound need have looked no further than Ernest Fenollosa's essay on Chinese poetry. Discussing metaphor, Fenollosa had said that "relations are more real and

more important than the things which they relate," and he went
on to suggest that there is an "identity of structure" between the
channels of communication in nature (e.g., in trees and rivers)
and those in human society.[9] This is very close to the position
which Pound took in canto 45, when he set a great many parts of
society into mutual relationship, and then asserted that the key
to social structure lay in the way in which economic patterns act
to shape the actual, physical communication between individuals. Like the magnetic field at the end of canto 74, which forces
steel dust into the shape of a rose, economic "forces" arrange
human beings into the ordered structure we call society. By
canto 94, Pound's pursuit of this insight had led him to question
the deeper patterning of nature itself:

> The clover enduring,
>   basalt crumbled with time.
> "Are they the same leaves?"

When even rock crumbles in time, the persistence of something
as fragile as a leaf is miraculous indeed, and yet what persists is
not the individual clover, but only its pattern—as apparently
insubstantial when compared to a leaf as a leaf is when compared
to a stone.

In a different form, this was the idea that had led Pound to
trace recurring patterns in history, permitting him to see Thomas
Jefferson and Sigismundo Malatesta, for example, as separate
manifestations of a single pattern. In the later cantos, Pound
simply followed that interest further, studying the deeper
structures of the green world which he had rediscovered at Pisa.
In canto 94 he uses an organic metaphor to suggest the way in
which great minds contain patterns of whole, complex perceptions ("to Mencius, Dante, and Agassiz/for Gestalt seed"). But
elsewhere he reverses the metaphor, as in canto 113, where he
notes that "there is something intelligent in the cherry-stone."
Pound's use of "intelligent" here is no accident, but rather part of
a fabric of belief which may be found throughout *The Cantos*.
The "bone luz" of canto 80 is associated with the "grain seed"
and refers to the belief in occult philosophy that from this small,
incorruptible bone, as from a seed, the resurrection of the body
will spring.[10] But *luz* mean "light," and light, mind. And for
Pound, light and mind rest in language: "mouth, is the sun that is

god's mouth" (canto 77). Thus when, near the end of *The Cantos*, he asks who can "enter the great acorn of light," he is speaking of learning to see in such a way that perception itself will be as an acorn, filled with invisible patterns capable of structuring the opaque world of matter.

In 1915, in *Gaudier-Brzeska: A Memoir*, Pound had mentioned an obscure seventeenth-century philosopher of the occult whose ideas about "pure form" had seemed especially relevant to the modernist art which Pound was discussing. Much later, in the *Rock-Drill Cantos*, that philosopher is mentioned again, this time with a title, "Secretary of Nature, J. Heydon." His reappearance in the later cantos is easily understood, given his belief in the possibility of learning to "read" the crucial messages which are imprinted within each living thing, determining its form: "oak leaf never plane leaf. John Heydon" (573). Like the intelligence of the cherry stone, there is a pattern of forces in every organism which shapes the common stuff of matter into innumerable distinct forms. And not only is the intricate structure of a plant contained invisibly in its seed, but the intelligence of man and beast is capable of penetrating the opaqueness of matter to read those "signatures," just as the "swallows eat cellandine" because they know the virtue of that plant. By the end of *The Cantos* Pound makes it clear that the light he too seeks might be read out of nature.

In canto 2 the entire crew of a ship, after sleighting Dionysus, is changed into fish, while in the late cantos Apollonius of Tyana, "who spoke to the lion" and "made peace with the animals," enters as a kind of Orpheus figure, communicating in perfect harmony with beasts of the forest. The poet who asks, in one of the last cantos, "can you see with the eyes of coral or turquoise/ or walk with the oak's root?" (777) is near the place where he began sixty years earlier (e.g., "The Tree"), and yet the meaning of that question is rendered far more complex by the explorations in between. Seeking after the nature of pattern, Pound had looked to Confucian thought, and what he found there only confirmed his earliest intuitions. In canto 99 he surveys a traditional Chinese civilization in which the sovereign "likes plowing," and the empress "tends trees with reverence," and his conclusion makes clear that a social wisdom such as this is no mere accident: "the plan is in nature/rooted" (709). Nor is it the result of "one man's mere power," but rather an imperative at the very heart of things. Pound's statement could not be more concise: "there is a must at the root of it." To acknowledge this truth is to join those Confucians who "observe the weather,/hear thunder,/seek to include." Like the story of the emperor Yu, praised because he could see ten lines of relationship where the ordinary man saw only one, Confucian thought as Pound rendered it perceives the universe whole.

When Pound began to write, profound changes were already underway in his society. And for the men and women living through those changes nothing could be more urgent than the need to find some coherence in the midst of social dislocation, philosophical doubt, and radical technological change. Pound's poetry was one of many answers to that need, and its achievement is that during years when a supposed "avant-garde" could only see meaningless fragmentation in the breakdown of the old order, it followed its vision of wholeness through decades of doubt and scorn. Even in their formal techniques, *The Cantos* embody a desire to seek new kinds of order which has moved far beyond the first shock of discovering *The Waste Land* at the end of a thousand years of culture. In the beginning, Pound thought that his long poem would end in a Paradiso, and the late cantos are indeed filled with images of light like those in Dante. At the end of a journey of mind unparalleled in modern verse, he did find a kind of paradise, though his need had only been, like Dante's, to learn to see it. When the vision came, his world was no less filled with pain and disorder than it had been when first hopes began to die in 1914. But through all the years of seeming failure, Pound had learned to see, and to record, what his age was slowly beginning to recover: its humble ground, its rootedness, its earth.

Notes and References

Chapter One

1. *Personae: The Collected Shorter Poems of Ezra Pound* (New York, 1926); hereafter cited in text as *P*.
2. Reprinted in *Literary Essays of Ezra Pound* (New York, 1968), p. 367.
3. *Confessions of a Young Man* (1888), quoted in *The Symbolist Poem*, ed. Edward Engelberg (New York, 1967), p. 299.
4. See K. K. Ruthven, *A Guide to Ezra Pound's Personae* (1926), (Berkeley, 1969), pp. 57f.; and Thomas H. Jackson, *The Early Poetry of Ezra Pound* (Cambridge, 1968), pp. 42f.
5. Quoted in C. K. Stead, *The New Poetic: Yeats to Eliot* (New York, 1964), p. 52. Stead offers a full discussion of the struggle against this prevailing literary atmosphere.
6. *Literary Essays*, p. 276.
7. Ibid., p. 277.
8. Ibid., p. 419.
9. *The Letters of Ezra Pound 1907-1941*, ed. D. D. Paige (New York, 1950), pp. 3f.
10. Ibid., p. 6.
11. K. K. Ruthven prints the entire note in his *Guide*, pp. 158f.

Chapter Two

1. *Letters*, p. 10.
2. Reprinted in *Ezra Pound: Selected Prose 1909-1965*, ed. William Cookson (New York, 1973), p. 102.
3. *Selected Prose*, p. 128.
4. "The Renaissance," reprinted in *Literary Essays*, p. 224.
5. Ibid., p. 232.
6. Introduction to *Ezra Pound: Translations* (New York, 1963), p. 9.
7. *The Metamorphic Tradition in Modern Poetry* (New Brunswick, N.J., 1955), p. 45.
8. "Osiris—Part I," *New Age* 10 (November 30, 1911), 107.

9. Translated by Kevin Crossley-Holland, in *The Battle of Maldon and Other Old English Poems*, ed. Bruce Mitchell (New York, 1967), pp. 118f.

10. *Ezra Pound and the Troubadour Tradition* (Princeton, 1972), pp. 36ff.

11. *The Spirit of Romance* (Norfolk, Conn., 1952), p. 166.

12. Ibid., p. 90.

13. Ibid., p. 94.

14. Ibid., pp. 92f.

15. Ibid., p. 101.

16. *Translations*, p. 19.

17. Ibid., p. 18.

18. "Cavalcanti," in *Literary Essays*, p. 150. This essay was not published until 1934, though parts of it were written as early as 1910.

19. *Selected Prose*, p. 58.

20. *Literary Essays*, p. 152.

21. Ibid., p. 153.

22. Ibid., p. 94.

23. K. K. Ruthven, in *A Guide to Ezra Pound's Personae*, gives the date as 1914 and therefore interprets "Provincia Deserta" as a record of that trip. Noel Stock's biography, *The Life of Ezra Pound* (New York, 1970), dates their tour as 1919.

Chapter Three

1. Michael Reck, *Ezra Pound: A Close-Up* (New York, 1967), p. 193.

2. *Selected Prose*, pp. 161f.

3. *Literary Essays*, p. 193.

4. Ruthven, *A Guide*, p. 204.

5. *Selected Prose*, p. 22.

6. *Letters*, p. 11.

7. *Literary Essays*, p. 3.

8. Ibid., p. 4.

9. *Selected Prose*, p. 49.

10. *Literary Essays*, p. 11.

11. *Selected Prose*, pp. 113f.

12. Some critics even see it as a regression in his work; see Donald Davie, *Ezra Pound: Poet As Sculptor* (New York, 1964), p. 33.

13. *Selected Prose*, p. 231.

14. Quoted in Ruthven, p. 153.

15. *Selected Prose*, p. 375.

16. *Literary Essays*, p. 220.

Chapter Four

1. H. A. Giles, *A History of Chinese Literature* (New York, 1901).
2. *The Chinese Written Character as a Medium for Poetry*, ed. Ezra Pound (1920; reprint San Francisco, n.d.), pp. 21f.
3. Ibid., p. 28.
4. Ibid., pp. 22f.
5. For a notion of what Pound had to work with, see the notes which are reproduced in Hugh Kenner, *The Pound Era* (Berkeley and Los Angeles, 1971), pp. 193ff.; and Wai-lim Yip, *Ezra Pound's Cathay* (Princeton, 1969).
6. This is one of the theses of Yip's book.
7. Introduction to *Ezra Pound: Selected Poems*, ed. T. S. Eliot (London, 1928).
8. *The Pound Era*, p. 202.
9. *Ezra Pound: Poet as Sculptor*, p. 25.
10. Not included in the original edition of *Cathay*, but published the following year (1916), and reprinted in the *Cathay* section of *Personae* (1926).
11. *Literary Essays*, p. 215.
12. Ibid., p. 224.

Chapter Five

1. Christine Brooke-Rose's response to these poems is typical of many critics who rather wish Pound had not written them at all; see *A ZBC of Ezra Pound*, p. 158.
2. Selected Prose, p. 120.
3. *The Life of Ezra Pound* (New York, 1970).
4. Quoted in J. P. Sullivan, *Ezra Pound and Sextus Propertius* (Austin, 1964), p. 6.
5. *Letters*, p. 148.
6. Ibid., p. 178.
7. See, for example, K. K. Ruthven, *A Guide*, p. 85.
8. Sullivan, p. 81.
9. *Letters*, p. 150. Orage was the editor of *The New Age*, where a good deal of Pound's writing was first published.
10. *Letters*, p. 231.
11. Sullivan, p. 33.

Chapter Six

1. *On Modernism: The Prospects for Literature and Freedom* (Cambridge, Mass., 1967), p. 38.

2. *Ezra Pound's Mauberley: A Study in Composition* (Berkeley and Los Angeles, 1955).

3. *The Spirit of Romance,* p. 3.

4. *Selected Prose,* p. 224.

5. Ibid., p. 120.

6. Ibid., p. 212

7. *Spirit of Romance,* p. 92.

8. *Selected Prose,* p. 118.

9. *Literary Essays,* p. 363.

10. Hugh Kenner has suggested that Max Beerbohm was Pound's model though John Espey has pointed out that Beerbohm was not a Jew. The question is not ultimately important, however, because the "Brennbaum" of Pound's poem *is* a Jew, and his significance is precisely that he has sacrificed that ancient heritage for the sake of an empty "respectability."

Chapter Seven

1. Quoted in Stock, *The Life of Ezra Pound,* p. 235.

2. Daniel D. Pearlman, *The Barb of Time: On the Unity of Ezra Pound's Cantos* (New York, 1969), p. 33. A similar point has been made by K. K. Ruthven, "Some New Approaches to Ezra Pound," *Southern Review* (Australia) 4 (1971), 308-15.

3. William Butler Yeats, *A Vision* (New York, 1966), p. 4.

4. *Letters,* p. 321.

5. Ibid., p. 210.

6. *Selected Prose,* p. 167.

7. Ibid., p. 90.

8. All references to *The Cantos* are to *The Cantos of Ezra Pound* (New York, 1970).

9. *Literary Essays,* p. 215.

10. *Selected Prose,* p. 285.

11. *Guide to Kulchur* (New York, 1938), p. 24.

12. "The Great Digest," reprinted with "The Unwobbling Pivot" and "the Analects" in *Confucius* (New York, 1969), p. 27.

13. Ibid., pp. 174f.

14. *The Poetry of Ezra Pound* (Norfolk, Conn., n.d.), p. 326.

15. Michael Reck, *Ezra Pound: A Close-Up,* p. 185.

16. *Guide to Kulchur,* p. 16.

Chapter Eight

1. *Selected Prose,* p. 169.

2. Ibid., p. 87.

3. *Guide to Kulchur*, p. 57.

4. *Selected Prose*, p. 284.

5. Buckminster Fuller, "Fluid Geography," in *Ideas and Integrities*, ed. Robert W. Marks (New York, 1969), pp. 119–41.

6. Marshall McLuhan, *Understanding Media: The Extensions of Man* (New York, 1965).

7. *The Analyst*, ed. Robert Mayo (Department of English, Northwestern University, n.d.); and John Edwards and William Vasse, *Annotated Index to the Cantos of Ezra Pound: Cantos I-LXXXIV* (Berkeley and Los Angeles, 1971).

8. *Ezra Pound: A Close-Up*, p. 198.

9. *Reading the Cantos: A Study of Meaning in Ezra Pound* (New York, 1966).

10. *Selected Prose*, p. 147.

Chapter Nine

1. William M. Chace, *The Political Identities of Ezra Pound and T. S. Eliot* (Stanford, 1973), p. 67.

2. Donald Davie sees this aspect of Pound's thought as central to the sometimes baffling range of style and subject matter in his verse, in *Ezra Pound: Poet as Sculptor*, p. 17.

3. *Spirit of Romance*, pp. 92f.

4. Gertrude Stein, *The Autobiography of Alice B. Toklas* (1933; reprint New York, 1960), p. 200.

5. This position is represented most unsparingly by Lilian Feder, *Ancient Myth in Modern Poetry* (Princeton, 1971).

6. Reported by Michael Reck in *Ezra Pound: A Close-Up*, p. 154.

7. *The Chinese Written Character*, p. 11.

8. *Steps to an Ecology of Mind* (New York, 1972), p. 153.

9. *The Chinese Written Character*, p. 22.

10. Boris de Rachewiltz, "Pagan and Magic Elements in Ezra Pound's Works," in *New Approaches to Ezra Pound*, ed. Eva Hesse (Berkeley, 1969), p. 191.

Selected Bibliography

For a full bibliography of Pound's writings, see GALLUP, DONALD. *A Bibliography of Ezra Pound*. London: Rupert Hart-Davis, 1966.

PRIMARY SOURCES

1. Poetry

A Lume Spento. Venice: A. Antonini, 1908. Reprint New York: New Directions, 1965.
A Quinzaine for this Yule. London: Pollock and Co., 1908.
Personae of Ezra Pound. London: Elkin Mathews, 1909.
Exultations of Ezra Pound. London: Elkin Mathews, 1909.
Provença. Boston: Small, Maynard and Co., 1910.
Canzoni of Ezra Pound. London: Elkin Mathews, 1911.
Ripostes. London: Swift and Co., 1912.
Cathay. London: Elkin Mathews, 1915.
Lustra. London: Elkin Mathews, 1916.
Lustra. New York: Alfred Knopf, 1917. Includes additional poems.
Quia Pauper Amavi. London: The Egoist Ltd., 1919.
Hugh Selwyn Mauberley. London: the Ovid Press, 1920.
Umbra. London: Elkin Mathews, 1920.
Poems 1918-1921. New York: Boni & Liveright, 1921.
A Draft of XVI Cantos. Paris: Three Mountains Press, 1925.
Personae: The Collected Poems of Ezra Pound. New York: Boni & Liveright, 1926.
Selected Poems. Edited, with introduction, by T. S. Eliot. London: Faber & Gwyer, 1928.
A Draft of XXX Cantos. Paris: Hours Press, 1930.
Eleven New Cantos XXXI-XLI. New York: Farrar & Rinehart Inc., 1934.
Alfred Venison's Poems: Social Credit Themes by the Poet of Tichfield Street. London: Stanley Nott, 1935.
The Fifth Decad of the Cantos XLII-LI. London: Faber & Faber, 1937.
Cantos LII-LXXI. Norfolk Conn.: New Directions, 1940.
A Selection of Poems. London: Faber & Faber, 1940.
The Pisan Cantos. New York: New Directions, 1948.
The Cantos [I-LXXXIV]. New York: New Directions, 1948.

Selected Poems. New York: New Directions, 1949.

The Translations of Ezra Pound. Introduction by Hugh Kenner. New York: New Directions, 1953.

The Classic Anthology Defined by Confucius. Translated by Ezra Pound. Cambridge: Harvard University Press, 1954.

Section: Rock-Drill, 85-95 de los cantares. New York: New Directions, 1956.

Sophokles: Women of Trachis, a version by Ezra Pound. New York: New Directions, 1957.

Diptych Rome-London: Homage to Sextus Propertius and Hugh Selwyn Mauberley. New York: New Directions, 1958.

Thrones: 96-109 de los cantares. New York: New Directions, 1959.

Love Poems of Ancient Egypt. Translated by Ezra Pound and Noel Stock. Norfolk, Conn.: New Directions, 1962.

Drafts and Fragments of Cantos CX-CXVII. New York: New Directions, 1969.

The Cantos of Ezra Pound. New York: New Directions, 1970.

Selected Cantos of Ezra Pound. New York: New Directions, 1970.

2. Prose

The Spirit of Romance. London: Dent & Son, 1910.

Gaudier-Brzeska: A Memoir. London: Bodley Head, 1916.

Certain Noble Plays of Japan. Introduction by W. B. Yeats. Churchtown, Dundrum, Ireland: The Cuala Press, 1916.

Pavannes and Divisions. New York: Alfred Knopf, 1918.

Instigations of Ezra Pound. New York: Boni & Liveright, 1920.

The Natural Philosophy of Love, by Remy de Gourmont. Translated, with introduction, by Pound. New York: Boni & Liveright, 1922.

Antheil and the Treatise on Harmony. Paris: Three Mountains Press, 1924.

Ta Hio, The Great Learning. An American version by Ezra Pound Seattle: University of Washington Book Store, 1928.

Imaginary Letters. Paris: The Black Sun Press, 1930.

How to Read. London: Desmond Harmsworth, 1931.

ABC of Economics. London: Faber & Faber, 1933.

ABC of Reading. London: Routledge & Sons, 1934.

Make It New. London: Faber & Faber, 1934.

Social Credit: An Impact. London: Stanley Nott, 1935.

Jefferson and / or Mussolini. London: Stanley Nott, 1935.

Polite Essays. London: Faber & Faber, 1937.

Guide to Kulchur. London: Faber & Faber, 1938.

Confucius: The Unwobbling Pivot and The Great Digest. Norfolk, Conn.: New Directions, 1947.

The Letters of Ezra Pound 1907–1941. Edited by D. D. Paige. New York: Harcourt Brace & Co., 1950.

Literary Essays of Ezra Pound. Selected, with introduction, by T. S. Eliot. Norfolk, Conn.: New Directions, 1954.

Pavannes and Divagations. Norfolk, Conn.: New Directions, 1958.

Impact: Essays on Ignorance and the Decline of American Civilization. Selected, with introduction, by Noel Stock. Chicago: Henry Regnery, 1960.

EP to LU: Nine Letters Written to Louis Untermeyer by Ezra Pound. Edited by J. A. Robbins. Bloomington: Indiana University Press, 1963.

Confucius to Cummings: An Anthology of Poetry. Edited by Ezra Pound and Marcella Spann. New York: New Directions, 1964.

Pound / Joyce—The Letters of Ezra Pound to James Joyce. Edited by Forrest Read. New York: New Directions, 1967.

Confucius: The Great Digest, The Unwobbling Pivot, The Analects. New York: New Directions, 1969.

Selected Prose 1909–1965. Edited, with introduction, by William Cookson. New York: New Directions, 1973.

SECONDARY SOURCES

BAUMANN, WALTER. *The Rose in the Steel Dust: An Examination of the Cantos of Ezra Pound.* Bern: Francke Verlag, 1967. Attempts to "show the Poundian centre" by focusing very specifically on cantos 4 and 82, and on the Odysseus motif.

BROOKE-ROSE, CHRISTINE. *A ZBC of Ezra Pound.* Berkeley: University of California Press, 1971. Many good insights, though not as introductory as it claims to be.

BUSH, RONALD. *The Genesis of Ezra Pound's Cantos.* Princeton: Princeton University Press, 1976. Detailed examination of the early drafts of the first few cantos.

CHACE, WILLIAM M. *The Political Identities of Ezra Pound and T. S. Eliot.* Stanford: Stanford University Press, 1973. Sees Pound as a radical as well as a reactionary, and attempts to understand the sources of his disastrous activism.

CORNELL, JULIEN. *The Trial of Ezra Pound.* New York: John Day, 1966. An account of Pound's trial, by his lawyer; heavily documented.

DAVIE, DONALD. *Ezra Pound: Poet as Sculptor.* New York: Oxford University Press, 1964. Deals with the poetry chronologically, emphasizing Pound's use of sources, and the technical achievement of his verse.

DAVIS, EARLE. *Vision Fugitive: Ezra Pound and Economics.* Lawrence: University of Kansas Press, 1968. Treats Pound's economic theories in the context of his life and his poetry.

DEKKER, GEORGE. *Sailing After Knowledge.* London: Routledge & Kegan Paul, 1963. Assumes that "certain cantos are a great deal better than others" and "should be isolated for special attention."

DEMBO, LAWRENCE. *The Confucian Odes of Ezra Pound, A Critical Appraisal.* Berkeley: University of California Press, 1963. Examines "the rhetorical methods used to render some of the major genres" in the *Classic Anthology.*

EDWARDS, JOHN HAMILTON and VASSE, WILLIAM V. *Annotated Index to the Cantos of Ezra Pound, Cantos I-LXXXIV.* Berkeley: University of California Press, 1957. Indispensable reference work for *The Cantos.*

EMERY, CLARK. *Ideas Into Action: A Study of Pound's Cantos.* Coral Gables, Fla.: University of Miami Press, 1958. Argues for the coherent structure of *The Cantos* by showing how its form issues directly from Pound's ideas.

ESPEY, JOHN J. *Ezra Pound's Mauberley: A Study in Composition.* Berkeley: University of California Press, 1955. An exhaustive study of the poem, employing "textual collation, identification of sources, and historical method."

HESSE, EVA, ed. *New Approaches to Ezra Pound.* Berkeley: University of California Press, 1969. A useful collection of essays by some of the best critics of Pound's work.

HEYMANN, C. DAVID. *Ezra Pound: The Last Rower. A Political Profile.* New York: Viking, 1976. Balanced account of Pound's political beliefs, drawing on previously unavailable F.B.I. files.

HOMBERGER, ERIC, ed. *Ezra Pound: The Critical Heritage.* London: Routledge & Kegan Paul, 1972. A collection of contemporary reviews of Pound's work; sheds light on the controversy which always accompanied his career.

JACKSON, THOMAS H. *The Early Poetry of Ezra Pound.* Cambridge: Harvard University Press, 1968. Traces the formation of Pound's poetics, "curiously complete almost from the very beginning," in his first few volumes of poetry.

KENNER, HUGH. *The Poetry of Ezra Pound.* Norfolk, Conn.: New Directions, n.d. One of the first (1951) major attempts at the exposition of Pound's verse, this is still a valuable book.

——. *The Pound Era.* Berkeley: University of California Press, 1971. Ambitious, and largely successful attempt to define some of the intellectual premises which Pound shared with his age.

LEARY, LEWIS, ed. *Motive and Method in the Cantos of Ezra Pound.* New York: Columbia University Press, 1954. Four essays dealing with the technique and some of the important themes in *The Cantos.*

McDOUGAL, STUART Y. *Ezra Pound and the Troubadour Tradition.* Princeton: Princeton University Press, 1972. The fullest examina-

172 EZRA POUND

tion of Pound's interest in the traditions, forms, and values of medieval troubadour verse.

MULLINS, EUSTACE. *This Difficult Individual, Ezra Pound.* New York: Fleet Publishing Company, 1961. Biographical study, emphasizing the years of Pound's trial and confinement at St. Elizabeth's.

DE NAGY, N. C. *The Poetry of Ezra Pound: The Pre-Imagist Stage.* Rev. ed. Bern: A. Francke A. G. Verlag, 1968. Studies the literary merit of Pound's early work, the influences which shaped it, and its relevance to *The Cantos.*

NASSAR, EUGENE PAUL. *The Cantos of Ezra Pound: The Lyric Mode.* Baltimore: The Johns Hopkins University Press, 1975. Argues for tragic duality in *The Cantos,* as fleeting moments of creative imagination are always set against the darker context of human history.

NORMAN, CHARLES. *The Case of Ezra Pound.* New York: Funk & Wagnalls, 1968. An account of Pound's trial, including testimony and documents.

———. *Ezra Pound.* Rev. ed. London: Macdonald, 1969. Full-length, generally sympathetic biography.

PEARLMAN, DANIEL D. *The Barb of Time: On the Unity of Ezra Pound's Cantos.* New York: Oxford University Press, 1969. Suggests that the question of whether *The Cantos* are possessed of "major form" may be answered by examining the coherent uses of time through the poem.

QUINN, SISTER BERNETTA. *Ezra Pound: An Introduction to the Poetry.* New York: Columbia University Press, 1972. A good place to begin reading about Pound and his poetry.

RECK, MICHAEL. *Ezra Pound: A Close-Up.* New York: McGraw-Hill, 1967. A good, brief portrait of Pound's life.

ROSENTHAL, M. L. *A Primer of Ezra Pound.* New York: Macmillan, 1960. Very brief introduction to the poetry.

RUTHVEN, K. K. *A Guide to Ezra Pound's Personae (1926).* Berkeley: University of California Press, 1969. Helpful explanatory notes to all the poems in *Personae.*

SCHNEIDAU, HERBERT N. *Ezra Pound: The Image and the Real.* Baton Rouge: Louisiana State University Press, 1969. Discusses Pound's poetics, particularly the problems associated with imagist theory and with Pound's attitudes toward a "reality" at times quite mystical.

STOCK, NOEL, ed. *Ezra Pound: Perspectives.* Chicago: Henry Regnery, 1965. Historical and critical essays, including letters from a number of writers.

———. *The Life of Ezra Pound.* New York: Pantheon Books, 1970. Full-scale biography, well documented with regard to the events of Pound's life, but not particularly interested in offering a sense of the private man and his emotions.

————. *Reading the Cantos*. New York: Pantheon Books, 1966. Argues that *The Cantos* do not constitute a coherent work, and that many passages are unsuccessful as poetry.

SULLIVAN, J. P. *Ezra Pound and Sextus Propertius: A Study in Creative Translation*. Austin: University of Texas Press, 1964. A close examination of Pound's use of his source, grappling with the question of how strictly the "Homage" should be judged as translation.

SUTTON, WALTER, ed. *Ezra Pound: A Collection of Critical Essays*. Englewood Cliffs, N. J.: Prentice-Hall, 1963. A useful, general selection of essays.

WATTS, HAROLD H. *Ezra Pound and the Cantos*. Chicago: Henry Regnery, 1952. Argues that "the concept at the heart of Pound's thought is that of 'ideas in action.' "

WILHELM, JAMES J. *Dante and Pound: The Epic of Judgment*. Orono: University of Maine Press, 1974. A detailed examination of Dante's important influence on Pound.

————. *The Later Cantos of Ezra Pound*. New York: Walker & Company, 1977. First book length examination of the later cantos.

WITEMEYER, HUGH. *The Poetry of Ezra Pound: Forms and Renewal 1908-1920*. Berkeley: University of California Press, 1969. Treats Pound's early writings, assuming that his later work "is often an elaboration of the concerns and dispositions of his youth."

YIP, WAI-LIM. *Ezra Pound's Cathay*. Princeton: Princeton University Press, 1969. Examines these poems as translations, and as new "forms of consciousness."

Index